AMIR KHAN

A Boy from Bolton: My Story

Amir Khan with Kevin Garside

BLOOMSBURY

First published in Great Britain 2006
This paperback edition published 2007

Copyright © 2006 by Amir Khan

The moral right of the author has been asserted

All photographs courtesy of the Khan family except where otherwise stated

Bloomsbury Publishing Plc,
36 Soho Square,
London W1D 3QY

A CIP catalogue record for this book
is available from the British Library

ISBN 9780747588054

10 9 8 7 6 5 4 3 2 1

Typeset by Hewer Text UK Ltd, Edinburgh
Printed in Great Britain by Clays Ltd, St Ives plc

All papers used by Bloomsbury Publishing are natural,
recyclable products made from wood grown in well-managed
forests. The manufacturing processes conform to the
environmental regulations of the country of origin.

www.bloomsbury.com/amirkhan

I dedicate this book to my late grandad and grandma, Lall Khan and Iqbal Begum, who made everything possible; and to my mum, dad, brother Haroon, sisters Tabinda and Mariyah, and my close family.

CONTENTS

FOREWORD BY BARRY McGUIGAN   ix

PROLOGUE   1

1. ROUND 1   7
2. ATHENS CALLING   30
3. WALLFLOWER TO POSTER BOY   60
4. ALL ROADS LEAD TO RAWALPINDI   77
5. FAREWELL TO KINDELAN   86
6. PUNCHING FOR PAY   103
7. I'M A CELEBRITY GET ME OUT OF HERE   120
8. KEEPING IT IN THE FAMILY   134
9. FIGHTING BACK THE TEARS   145
10. LICENCE TO THRILL   157
11. BOYZ IN THE HOOD   163
12. 7 JULY 2005   177

ACKNOWLEDGEMENTS   189
CAREER RECORD   191
INDEX   201

Foreword

by Barry McGuigan

I've seen a lot of young boxers in my day. In the past fifteen years working full time as a TV commentator for Sky and ITV, I've seen every hot prospect to emerge on both sides of the Atlantic. Amir Khan is as good as any I've witnessed, as good as Floyd Mayweather Jnr, as good as Oscar De La Hoya. I don't say that lightly. I don't want to make Amir's job harder than it already is by damning him with faint praise, especially these days when the transition from amateur to pro is as hard as it has ever been. More and more the amateur and professional codes are becoming almost separate disciplines. Sure, they take place in a ring and the boxers wear shorts, but that's about the only similarity in the twenty-first century. Not so long ago an Olympic medal was almost a guarantee of success as a pro. Floyd Patterson, Muhammad Ali, Joe Frazier, Sugar Ray Leonard, Lennox Lewis all went on to win world titles. Nowadays most major amateur crowns are won by tall, rangy boxers, often southpaws. That's no accident. The amateur code, with its head guards, bigger, cushioned gloves, shorter rounds and questionable scoring system, promotes a kind of in-and-out technique. You tap and go. Boxers become almost institutionalised, making the crossover to fighting for three minutes a round on the inside within punching distance wearing smaller gloves harder than ever to make. Witness the struggle that Audley Harrison has endured. Amir is exceptional. I won Commonwealth gold at seventeen. That was hard enough. To challenge one of the greatest amateur boxers of all time, a Cuban double Olympic gold medallist, and push him all the way in an Olympic final defied belief. To then come back from that and beat Mario Kindelan in what turned out to be the last amateur bout for both demonstrated the vast depth of Amir's talent.

To get on in this game you need many qualities. Uppermost is attitude. Without the right approach a boxer cannot hope to sustain the kind of commitment required to train hard and prepare properly for fights in a long career. They call boxing the truth game. If there are any weaknesses or corners cut, it finds you out in the end. Amir's attitude is first class. He loves to fight, and he listens. Six months into his pro career I went up to Manchester to film a session with Amir at Oliver Harrison's gym in Salford. We did some pad work, hit the speed ball, the usual stuff, then when the cameras had gone, we sat on the ring apron and had a chat. There were only a few people in the gym: me, Amir, Oliver and Steve Foster Jnr. We talked boxing. You would not have known Amir was there. He never said a word. As an amateur, he had achieved more than any of us. Here, he was just soaking up everything, tucking it away to measure against his own experience down the road.

There are no guarantees in sport. But if any fighter has a chance it is Amir, in my opinion the most important British boxer to emerge in a generation. He has all the attributes required to scale the highest peaks as a pro, just as he did as an amateur, to go on to achieve his ambition of a world title. But his appeal is broader than sport. He has universal appeal, crossing over so many boundaries, whether it be race, religion or creed. The present political climate, at home and abroad, has placed Amir, a boy from Bolton, in a delicate position. Yet he does honour to his Pakistani roots and his Muslim faith while at the same time being as British as any in this sceptred isle. I know a little about upheaval in times of political turbulence. I had to fight during one of the most troubled times in Irish history. As an Irish Catholic from a town in the Republic I fought for the British title. I married a Protestant at a time when people were losing their lives as a result of their religious orientation, just as they are now in Amir's era. It wasn't my fault. It's not Amir's. He has handled the situation with honesty, integrity and sincerity, displaying a measure of maturity way beyond his years. He did not acquire those qualities overnight. Like me, he grew up in a loving family, among genuine people. The result is a humble boy devoid of artifice. He has every reason to shout from the roof-tops, yet he remains free of arrogance. His humility is refreshing in the age of the sporting megastar. This is what makes Amir so special.

The temptations are many for today's sporting heroes. You need to stay true to yourself. That takes discipline, hard work and character, qualities that Amir has in abundance.

Think about all those eight-, nine-, ten-year-olds who watched Amir win the silver medal in Athens. They were already con-nected to him when he switched codes to join the professional ranks. He will be part of their lives for ever as a consequence of that remarkable Olympic Odyssey. As a paid-up member of the boxing community, I'm honoured to say that Amir Khan will for ever be a part of my life too.

Barry McGuigan
Faversham, Kent
August 2006

Prologue

I'm sitting on the sofa in the front room of the new house. The extension has just been finished. It's a bungalow so it gives us a bit more space. My chest is aching from the gym session in the morning. Oliver, my trainer, has introduced some strength work. He had me bench-pressing 40 kilos for fifty reps. And that was just the warm-up.

I'm flicking through a car magazine. I like the look of the Mercedes CLR. My brother Haroon is watching the World Cup on TV with Taz, my uncle, and my dad. It's 15 June, England are playing Trinidad and Tobago. It's a rubbish match. Then Wayne Rooney starts walking up and down. He's about to make his World Cup debut seven weeks after breaking his foot. The papers have been talking about nothing else for weeks. It makes me smile. I am pleased for the lad. I've met him a couple of times. He seems like a nice guy. A couple of days earlier I was reading in one paper that I had been beaten as an amateur by Rooney's brother or cousin. I can't remember which. It wasn't true. I lost only nine times in the amateurs. I can remember the names of every opponent who beat me. There are none of the Rooney clan in that list. A lot of what is written about me in the papers isn't true. The sports stuff is fine, it's the other stuff that gets you, the girlfriends, the parties. I wish I had been out with half the girls I've been linked with. People can easily get the wrong impression. A friend of a friend's daughter asked him if I had a sister called Jemima. I'd been turned into the brother of Jemima Khan, the ex-wife of Imran. That's how mad it can get and one of the reasons I chose to write this book. People say I'm too young at nineteen to be writing an autobiography. They are absolutely right. This is not my autobiography. It is the first chapter in the story of my life.

So much has happened to me in the two years since I qualified for the Olympic Games in Athens. My life has changed beyond belief. If newspapers and magazines think I'm worth writing about, I reckon that there must be people out there who want to know about the real me, what I'm like, where I'm from, who I am.

In a way it's an ordinary story. Working-class lad from the North makes it big through sport. There are plenty of examples of kids like me who have done that. What makes my story unique is my background. I'm British, Bolton born and bred. But my ancestry is Asian, Pakistani. I'm a Muslim. That makes all the difference. There were no Asian lads boxing when I started. There aren't many now. I have never faced another Asian lad in the ring or appeared on the same bill with one. Personally it's not an issue. I have never felt victimised because of my background. And I have never fought for any cause other than my own. I'm not political. I'm not on a crusade. This story is about me, how I got started, what I had to do to get on, and eventually how I made it all the way to the Olympics just six years after my first amateur fight. But if one kid, whether from an Asian background or otherwise, picks up the gloves after reading my story, then I will have given something back, opened a door for someone else to step through.

And that's not all. Since 9/11 and the London bombings in July 2005, just a few days before my professional debut, the spotlight has been on Asian people everywhere. I spoke out against the bombings at the time. What those lads did shocked me. It had nothing to do with my faith as I understand it. I hope that after reading this book those who know little about the Muslim religion and what it means to follow the teachings of Islam in Britain will feel more comfortable with their Asian neighbours. It is a force for good not harm. But you would not know that judging by the coverage Muslims get in the media. It tends to be negative stuff. When it is about me it is almost always positive. That's very important for the Asian community in Bolton and the rest of the country.

On the wall behind me is a picture of my grandad and grandma with their four kids not long after they arrived in England. My grandad, Lall Khan, came from a village called Matore, near Rawalpindi, in 1963 with nothing. His first job was planting potatoes in Bradford. He had no idea when he posed for that picture what he had started. You'll learn all about him in this book.

Boxing has given me everything I have, the nice house, cars, holidays abroad. It has given me the chance to provide for my family in a way I could never have done otherwise. It has kept me off the streets, kept me from the kind of life that other lads like me live every day in Bolton. There are kids running about doing drugs, getting into trouble with the police, all sorts of stuff. I could have been one of them if my dad had not taken me to a boxing gym at eight years old.

Coping with fame and fortune as a teenager after winning a silver medal in Athens is another part of the story that I wanted to tell. I've had some amazing experiences, been to places that are not normally open to teenagers from Bolton, never mind Asian kids. It's not all rosy. There are pitfalls too. It would be very easy to get carried away with the celebrity lifestyle. I have my family and friends to thank for keeping my feet on the ground. You'll meet them in these pages too.

Crouch scores. Amazing! England look like a different team with Rooney on the pitch. Haroon goes mad. He's the footballer in the family. But like me he only has eyes for boxing. We have got high hopes for him. I hope he gets the chance to shine as I did. A year into my pro career, I realise how privileged I am. I'm getting paid for my hobby, doing what I love. That only happens to the odd few. I have travelled a long way. I never imagined it would feel this good to be a pro boxer. I've had seven fights. Seven tough fights. I have improved with every one. After my first fight I was rated 400-plus in the world. Twelve months on I've shot up to fifty-nine. As I look forward I feel that I'm at the start of an exciting new chapter in my life. British titles, European titles and hopefully world titles lie ahead. Maybe a year from now I'll be sat on the same sofa wearing my first championship belt.

Steven Gerrard makes it 2–0. Taz points to the England shirt that I'm wearing. It was given to me the day before at a press conference in Cardiff to announce amongst other fights my eighth bout as a professional, against Colin Bain. He's a Scottish lad. I don't know much about him. Come fight night I'll know every punch in his armoury. The shirt has got my initials on the shoulder in gold, a good colour. You'll have to wear that every time England play from now on. It must be a lucky shirt, Taz said. I remembered what my teacher Graham always used to tell the students at Bolton Community College: you make your own luck.

On the flight back from Cardiff – yes, we fly everywhere if we can, it saves so much time – the seating got a bit mixed up. The hostess told us to sit anywhere and if people needed to change seats we could do that in the air. An older couple got on. The woman wasn't best pleased to be in a different seat from that indicated on her ticket. My dad apologised. As she was sitting down she noticed me sitting next to my dad. Here, I know you, she said. You're that boxer, aren't you? You're Amir Khan and you are sitting in my seat. Before you get off I want your autograph for my grandson. No problem. I signed my boarding card and gave that to her. She was buzzing. That's how it's been since the Olympics. People of all ages, backgrounds and colour have connected with me. I must be doing something right.

On the way back to Bolton from Manchester airport I got a text from a mate telling me about a story on the boxing website Seconds Out. I know the bloke who writes most of the stuff, Clive Bernath. Nice guy. Seconds Out received a letter from a young boxer called Michael Grant, the lad I might have fought in the 2005 ABA (Amateur Boxing Association) finals if I hadn't withdrawn in a dispute over tickets. Michael was putting it about that the real reason I pulled out of the competition was because I didn't want to fight him, I was scared to face him. Yeah, right.

This is what he wrote in his letter:

I hereby state that as soon as I win my first title, and I shall be going down the road of legitimate titles, not jumping on the alphabet bandwagon of 'snide' titles, I will offer Khan the first voluntary defence. Perhaps if he should win a title he could do the same. I would be happy to box Khan. Khan holds no worries for me. I think he is less effective since he turned pro and he is not a thinking fighter.

Everyone is entitled to an opinion. Most people wait to be asked for theirs. The truth is almost a year to the day that I turned professional a boxer used my name to get publicity for himself. I'm surprised it took Michael so long. He must have hired Don King. He said his letter was a response to a piece about me in the trade paper *Boxing News*. In it I was supposedly quoted saying that Michael wasn't up to much. Very convenient. I'll get to Michael in good time. When it suits me, not him.

I've never been frightened of anybody in my life, never run away from a fight. I've been in the ring with Mario Kindelan, one of the greatest amateur boxers of all time. I won Olympic silver at seventeen, sometimes fighting against men almost twice my age. I have earned respect the hard way. Next time you write a letter, Michael, send it to me. There is too much disrespect shown between fighters in the professional game. You don't see much of that in the amateurs. It's better for it. Boxing is a sport after all.

The final whistle blows. The score is 2–0 to England. Cheers all round. As the players leave the pitch the doorbell goes. It's the physio. Another session in the torture chamber coming up. It's a price I'm happy to pay. Let's get on with it. Places to go . . .

1

Round 1

I couldn't tell you what makes the ideal fighter. All I know is that I've had fighting spirit in me for as long as I can remember. I never let anyone get away with anything. If anybody did anything to me they got it back, no messing. I was always in trouble. Not serious stuff, just running around, fighting with my cousins, getting told off. I was a handful as a kid, high-spirited, that's all. Everything changed when I started boxing. I channelled all my energies into that. I loved everything about it, the training, the pads, the bags and, best of all, the fighting. Before that all my energies went into mischief. Eight years of mischief.

Perhaps I was just making the most of a life that was almost over before it started. A couple of weeks after I was born, I was back in hospital with some sort of chest infection. At first they thought it was pneumonia. I was wrapped in tin foil, a special blanket to keep my temperature constant. My uncle Taz reckoned I looked like a chicken. I had a serious condition. My parents thought I wouldn't make it. I was tiny, stuck in an incubator in intensive care with tubes and needles keeping me alive. Maybe that has something to do with the way I turned out. Though I recovered well enough the family always felt a certain way towards me, giving me everything I wanted, spoiling me, I suppose, particularly my gran, Iqbal Begum. I thought

I could do whatever I wanted, when I wanted, that sort of attitude.

My parents were very strong on learning right from wrong. The thing was, I only paid attention when it suited me. My sisters Tabinda and Mariyah, and my brother Haroon are a lot calmer than me. More chilled. Most of the time they did as they were told. I was a bit more headstrong. We are a very close family.

Like a lot of immigrants from Pakistan my grandad, Lall Khan, came to England to make a better life. He came to Bolton on his own and set about earning enough money to pay for my grandmother to come over with their children. My dad, Shah, was nine years old when he arrived. At first they settled into the Pakistani community in Church Street. That was normal. But as soon as they could afford it, the family moved to another area where the neighbours were all English. My grandad taught his kids to respect everyone no matter what colour they were, or what religion they belonged to. He knew that to get on his children would have to settle into the English way of life quickly. It worked. If you speak to my dad now he can hardly remember anything of his childhood in Pakistan.

I grew up thinking everybody was the same. I didn't notice the colour of my skin. I did not think we were different or unusual. I was just Amir, running in and out of neighbours' houses like any other kid. That's how it has always been with me. Obviously I know about racism. But it has never been a problem for me or my family. I see myself as a Lancashire lad from Bolton, not as an outsider. So do my dad, my uncles, my aunts, my cousins. My dad had a car repair garage, then a breakers' yard, my uncle Shahid, known to family and friends as Terry, is a policeman, Uncle Tahir, known as Taz, an IT expert. Normal stuff. I'm proud of my Pakistani heritage. We all are. But I'm British.

Having survived the infection that left me hospitalised, one of my earliest memories is being hit by a car, a white Volvo. I'll never forget that car. We were at a wedding. All my cousins were messing about outside. Sajid, who plays cricket for Lancashire and England, and his brother, Rakeb. They legged it across the road into a park. I was about four years old. I didn't bother looking. I ran after them, like kids do. The next thing I knew I was on the floor. It felt like the Volvo had run over my leg. The flesh was just hanging there. The poor driver was in shock. He never had a chance. I was rushed to hospital. They sent me home the same day. Though they said I would be OK, there were some concerns that the leg might end up shorter than the other. I had to keep doing stretching exercises to make sure it healed properly. That was so painful. Everybody came around to the house, fussing over me, especially my gran. It was great. I made the most of it as usual.

Another time I threw my sister Tabinda's bike down a small ramp about 20 metres long. I don't know why I did it. Maybe I was trying to see how far it would go without anybody riding it. It ran out into the road on a blind bend. A car crashed into it. That meant more trouble. Not from the driver. He couldn't catch me. I legged it. But Mum and Dad weren't impressed. I must have been about six. They grounded me. That used to kill me. I was never in the house as a kid. To be stuck inside when all my mates and cousins were playing outside was torture to me.

They thought it would teach me a lesson. It never did. It just moved the trouble inside. When my uncle Taz wasn't looking I used to drink his orange juice then fill the container with tap water. I remember him telling my mum not to buy it again because it was really weak. That cracked me up. He didn't know. It was only when my mum caught me red-handed that he found out.

I didn't do things by the rules because I didn't recognise them. Or didn't want to. I had no idea about fear. I wasn't scared of anything. When I was five I climbed on top of the house. First I climbed on to a wall, then up the drainpipe. There I was, sitting on the roof. I could climb anything. I think I must have been the first base jumper in Bolton. My gran would be stood at the bottom telling me to get down. I loved it. I stayed up there for ages until she said she would tell my dad when he came home. I knew what that meant. No playing out. That scared me more than anything. I was down like a shot.

That fearless streak serves me well in boxing, but it was a nuisance for others, particularly my teachers. My parents had to move me out of one nursery school because the teachers couldn't handle me any more. They had had enough. Once I ate a piece of cake that was on the teacher's desk. I saw it sitting there for ages. I fancied it so I just went up and grabbed it for myself. My view was that the teacher shouldn't have left it there. But it wasn't her view and she told my mum that when she came to pick me up. I was a hyper-active kid, an absolute nightmare for the teachers. They got so fed up at one point that they said I could only stay at the school if a parent or guardian stayed too. My gran got the job. Being my gran she saw only the good in me. She told my parents that I was a good boy, it was all the fault of the other kids. There was an incident over a bike. According to Gran it wasn't my fault. I was sitting on the bike nicely, then some other kids would come over and take it off me. It happened again. Gran told me if it happened once more not to let them have it. That was the green light for me. When they tried to get the bike a third time I went mad. The teacher came over with a look on her face that said, told you so. My gran told the teacher that she didn't think I was to blame. I think the teacher tried to point out that if Gran wasn't there, I wouldn't have wasted any time seeking retribution. And it was never my fault. That was more or less the end of my days at Brownlow Fold. I changed schools shortly after that.

I started to get a reputation as a tough kid. No one messed with me. I never let anyone bully me. If they tried to take advantage they would get it. I used to get in fights all the time. A lot of kids did. It was normally with older brothers who would come around to try to sort me out. I might have got into some kind of scuffle with a lad my age and the next thing his brother or cousin would turn up. I didn't care what size they were. It was all the same to me. They'd get an early version of the right hand over the top. It was never nasty. I never started things. I just couldn't walk away. I had to fight my corner. Whenever the phone rang at home and I wasn't in, my dad just reached for his coat and car keys, ready to come and rescue me from one scrape or another. Then one day, out of the blue, my dad came home from work and asked if I would like to go to a boxing gym.

Looking back, it was an obvious step. Parents worry about their kids. My mum and dad were obviously concerned about me. They needed to channel my energy in a positive way. It must have been frustrating for them. Basically I was a good kid. I had good values. I knew the difference between right and wrong. But I was getting a reputation. It was probably the best decision my dad has ever made, or will ever make. It changed the course of my life, of all our lives.

We had no idea how things would turn out. I was only eight years old. I wasn't sure about it at first. And there was serious opposition from my mum and Gran. They did not want me to get bashed up. They had visions of me coming home with a broken nose, all beat up. My dad, my uncles, they all lied. They said they used to do it when they were kids. I'd love it, they said. It sparked my competitive instinct. I thought that if they had done it, so would I, only I'd be better. So off we went to Halliwell Boxing Club in Bolton. From the moment I walked through the doors I never threw another punch in the street. My tearaway days were over.

I can remember that first time as if it were yesterday. It was in the basement of an old factory. You walked down some narrow steps that turned to the left halfway down. It was dark and dusty, full of old leather bags tied up with chains. These days the bags are secured with proper leather straps. The ring was disgusting. The canvas had blood all over it. The gloves were all old. The place was a mess. And the smell, all stale and sweaty. It stank. I learned to love that smell. You could take me blindfold anywhere in the world and I could pick out a boxing gym at 100 paces. Soon as I get the scent, I feel at home.

People were hitting the bags, sparring, shadow boxing in front of mirrors. The place was kicking. The man who ran it was called Tommy Battle, a great name for a boxing coach. He was my first. In the beginning I wondered why all these people were skipping. I thought that was girlie stuff. And why were they hitting bags? Why weren't they hitting each other? When I got into it I just wanted to be better than the lad next to me. I think I had a go at everything that first night, except sparring. I paid my 50p subs and went for it. The gloves were massive. They felt funny. Tommy tied them on with shoe laces. I loved it.

At first I went twice a week. I would have gone every day if I could have done. I started to buy my own stuff, skipping rope, gloves. My first pair were white, really flash. I was the youngest there. But you would never have known it. The only thing they would not let me do was spar. I was too young. They kept me waiting at least a year before I got in the ring with another lad. Because I was the youngest and smallest, I was sparring with lads a lot heavier than me. I didn't care. I got hit but it didn't scare me. I just hit them back, sorted them out.

The only thing that did throw me was my first sight of blood. I was sparring with this lad and I bust him up. Blood everywhere. It got me a bit worried. My first thought was that I might be in trouble. What have I done here? I shouldn't have hit him that hard. I used to hit people to the body, never the face. Oh no, his mum and dad might come to my house. I might get arrested. All these thoughts were rushing around my head. The coach came up, said well done. I thought, great, I can do it again. That was it. He gave me permission to hit somebody. At home I was always being told that it was wrong to hit people. In the gym I was being encouraged to do it. It was a bit confusing in the beginning. In my first few sparring sessions I was thinking should I hit this lad or not? I was scared to hit people in the face. When they did it to me, I responded instinctively. Drawing blood was a big turning point for me. Once that had happened the chains were off. I had no more second thoughts. I was on my way.

It might seem hard to believe looking at me now, but I was chubby as a kid, short and fat. I used to sit there thinking I would never get a six-pack. Puppy fat, they called it. I was flat-footed, too. I never used to box people in the gym. I was a come forward slugger. I used to come out swinging, Tyson style. One day, Tommy Battle pulled me to one side. He put his thumbs under the heels of my boots and said, stand on them and you are dead. From that day on I stayed on my toes. Now I'm known for my footwork. People see that as one of my strengths. Back then, with my no. 1 haircut, I was more like a battering ram.

I used to eat and sleep boxing. When I wasn't at the gym I would train at home, watch videos. The *Rumble in the Jungle* was my favourite. I'd watch anything. Boxing was new to me and I wanted to learn, to see how other fighters did it. Muhammad Ali was my favourite. Every time I went to the gym I was Ali, dancing, moving, hitting.

After a year or so the Halliwell Boxing Club closed down. Tommy set up a new gym at Bolton Lads Club, a kind of after-school club for youngsters. I followed suit but they would not let me fight. They said I was too young. I was gutted. I started doing karate instead. You could kick there as well as punch. On the first day a girl punched me in the face. With her knuckles as well. I was stunned. I was also mad. I couldn't hit her back. She was a girl. I would never hit a girl. We moved along in a line to another partner. I battered him because of that punch. He was a tough lad as well, as good at karate as I was at boxing. People were amazed that I beat him up.

I did not go back to a boxing gym for more than a year. We

13

couldn't find one that would take me. They all said I was too young. I used to keep up the training at home, hitting the pads and stuff. Then when I was coming up to eleven, I went back to Bolton Lads Club. They would not take kids younger than eleven so my dad had a chat with Tommy Battle and he sorted it out for me to start training there.

I had my first amateur fight three days after my eleventh birthday, December 1997. It was in Stoke-on-Trent. I went down with my dad and my uncles Taz and Terry. I was so excited when I came out of school. I was going to have my first fight as a boxer. We had no idea what to expect. We had never been to a competition before. We bought a camcorder to record the moment. All my early fights are now on video. Whenever somebody comes to the house for the first time, they have to sit through them. Taz filmed everything that moved. The camera was a big thing, nothing like the hand-held things we have today. A full VHS videotape would fit inside.

It was a dinner show. We walked in and the place was full of skinheads drinking pints. I swear they all had tattoos. We were the only Asian family there. I was still a chubby thing then, short and fat. My opponent was massive. Mark Jones was his name, from a place called Atherstone. I'll never forget that name. I was warming up downstairs. My dad was a bit concerned at the size of him. Very tall he was compared to me. He'd had two or three fights already. I told Dad I was OK. I wasn't bothered at all. Most kids my age were taller than me then. One more wasn't going to make any difference. I had to wait for about an hour before I went on. I couldn't wait to get at him. I was wearing a yellow robe and vest from the Bolton Lads Club, and big blue gloves. There was a loud cheer when we got in the ring. The referee was called John Hart. He was dressed from head to toe in white. There was a bit of a wait until the judges had taken their seats. My dad was hovering in the corner. Taz was ready to go with the camera. Terry was smoking his head off in the background.

I hit him with some sweet shots. You could hear it on the camera afterwards. It was like the air whooshing out of a bag every time I hit him. The crowd went wild. We were like a pair of windmills in there, arms flailing. I tried to remember the disciplines, jab and move. But in that first thirty seconds it was chaos, whack, whack, whack. There were only three ninety-second rounds. At the end of every round I was shattered. I was taking some shots, too. I never felt one. I have always been comfortable in punching range. That is one of the reasons that later on I was able to make the transition from amateur to pro. My coach that night was called Tony. At the end of the first round he told me I was doing well, to keep my hands up and keep moving. We both started to tire in the second round. I started off throwing a few haymakers. After that I calmed down a bit, tried to move properly, jab, right hand over the top in a blue blur. I got it right a couple of times. It felt like I was a proper fighter. I caught him again with a left and a right, backed him up a few times. By the third round Mark was struggling a bit. I was catching him with some good shots. I landed a great uppercut towards the end. Even then I had all the shots. It was over in no time. I won on points. Mark was gutted. When he took his gloves off I noticed that his hands were taped up. We hadn't thought to put tape on mine.

Afterwards I was presented with a massive trophy to keep. Loads of people came up to my dad and uncles and said that they had a special boy there. It felt great, all these strangers telling me how good I was. I got a real buzz out of it. I thought, yeah, this is the sport for me. I was hooked. Six years after my amateur debut in Stoke-on-Trent I was fighting in Athens against Mario Kindelan for Olympic gold. It barely seems possible when you think about it. There was no thought of this thing going anywhere. I was just enjoying myself. My dad was happy that I'd found a hobby that I liked and that kept me out of trouble.

Right from the start I had the support of my family. My dad

and uncles came to all the fights. We were a real team. Without them there is no way I could have progressed. To get on you need to fight. There is no substitute for being in the ring. The shows were all over the country, midweek as well as weekends. Never once did I say no when the phone rang. Amir, do you fancy fighting tomorrow night? Where? Ipswich. No problem. We'd pile into the car, my uncle Taz carrying the massive camera, and off we would go.

After that first fight everyone was really proud. My confidence soared. My second fight was in February 1998 in Rawtenstall. I had a huge following from Bolton. Everyone I knew came to that fight. My cousin Saj was there, my old mate Maj. It was packed. I was in the blue corner for that fight, blue vest and shorts. John Hart was the referee again. I was fighting a lad called Gary Hart, no relation. It was just as well. I battered the lad from the start. He was about a foot taller than me. I just laid into him. You could tell he didn't fancy it. In the corner Taz was screaming throw the uppercut all the time. I didn't hear a thing in the ring. It's funny when I watch them now. No wonder the camera was all over the place. Taz was in there swinging like me. I kept catching him with combinations. I even threw the double jab. In my second fight! I had this habit of tapping the gloves together before I threw a punch. The lad should have read it but he didn't. Tap, tap, boom! That was how the fight went. Tap, tap, boom! The head guard I was wearing was not AIBA (Association of International Amateur Boxing) approved. I wore it for ages until I was pulled in Liverpool and told to get a proper one. I didn't need it in that second fight. Again I got a huge trophy. I had to pose for Taz, who took his job as cameraman seriously.

The third fight was the same. It was a month later at Kendall in the Lake District. I was in with a lad from Cleethorpes, Jack Morley. He was from a travelling family. I was all over him, backing him up in the corner. The referee told me to keep my head up. I caught him with a brilliant left. The lad started to spew up. I had made him sick. The referee had to mop it up. The second round was just the same. His family were going berserk, shouting. Use the jab, Jackie, use the jab. Come on. Jackie perked up a bit. I was still taking lumps out of him. The lad spewed up again. That was it. The fight was over. I'd stopped my first opponent in only my third fight. I thought that I'd broken his tooth, as well. I often wonder what happened to those lads I fought early on. They are out there somewhere, doing something. It would be cool to check them out again.

By now I was getting so confident. But at the same time I did not think I was getting the attention I needed to perform better. The training sessions were all over the place. I would have one coach come in and tell me this, another the next week would tell me that. The matchmaking wasn't very good either. At that age it is dead easy to mismatch boxers. It is done on a combination of age, weight and experience. I ended up going in against bigger lads with miles more experience. Surprise, surprise I lost my fourth fight, and my fifth, and my sixth.

The first defeat of my career was against a lad called Mark Unsworth from Liverpool. The fight was in April 1998 in front of Mark's own supporters in Liverpool. It was a genuine loss. I had no complaints. He was more experienced. He was taller than me and better organised. I had not come up against a lad as technical as him. After he had withstood the early thrash, he seemed to read all my moves. I stuck with it but I never felt that I was in the fight. He had more stamina than me. I felt tired that night. I was blowing. You always feel more tired when you are losing. Taz was screaming from the side, come on, Amir. I just didn't have it that night. For every punch I landed I took two in return. I was gutted. We met four times after that. I lost the next one, too, though my dad thought I had won it. Then I beat him three times on the spin. After the last defeat, Unsworth retired.

Next up was a lad called Palmer from Chorley. The fight was at Old Trafford, Manchester United's ground. It should never have taken place. He was much heavier than me. When he got in the ring I thought he must have been stood on a box. He was massive compared to me. I was looking a bit ragged. I couldn't make any impression on the lad. He was just too big. The coach should not have let it go ahead. He should have pulled me out before the start. Palmer had arms like pistons. I was in his face but making no headway. Afterwards, Jack Duckworth off *Coronation Street* came up to me and said well done for not giving up. I showed heart that night. I was gutted to lose again.

The next fight was in Middleton, Manchester. I walked out to the tune of *Rocky*. Even Rocky would have struggled against Ben Yates. He was eighteen months older than me, from the same club in Chorley as Palmer. You have to be within eleven months of your opponent at that level. Again he was so much bigger than I was. It was a close fight. I lost on a majority decision. The point is I should not have been in the ring with the lad in the first place. Yates had shoulders like Arnold Schwarzenegger. It was like Rocky *v* Ivan Drago. I caught him with a beautiful left. He lost his gum shield. Come on, Amir. That's all you could hear from the side. Taz got really excited. I battled on. I took a few shots. Keep battling, Taz was shouting. I never gave up, never stopped swinging. I'll never forget those blue-striped shorts Yates and Palmer wore. When we discovered that they were older than me, out of my age group, it meant that I was never able to fight them again. They were the only defeats that I have not avenged. Every other fighter that I lost to, and there were only seven others, I beat when we met again.

After that my dad said, right, that's it. Time for another gym. We tried a place in Manchester. No good. They only took pros. We had heard about an amateur club in Bury run by Mick Jelley. Mick had seen me in the fight against Yates. He thought I had bottle. So I got in the car with Dad and we drove over to Bury. We couldn't find it. We tried everywhere, up this street, down another. We asked people, still no joy. We had to go home and start again the next day.

No wonder we couldn't find it. When we eventually stumbled on it, in Willow Street, Bury, it was like a shed. When it rained, and it rained a lot in Bury, the gym would spring leaks. Mick used to try to dry out the light sockets by spraying them with WD40. If ever there was a problem with anything, Mick would get out the WD40. Within seconds it would be like Blackpool illuminations. The lights started arcing and the fuses blew. Apart from that it was a brilliant little club. Like every other amateur club in the country it relied on goodwill to survive. In our case the goodwill was Mick's. Mick is in his sixties. He has run Bury ABC for forty years. Before that his dad ran it. His dad was a good amateur, so were Mick's brothers. One of them, Peter, fought more than 400 times, one of them on the same bill as the great American heavyweight Joe Louis. Not many Englishmen can say they did that. That's proper boxing history. Peter lives in Canada now. He's always asking Mick how I'm doing. He can't get my name right. How's the Aga Khan? he says.

Under Mick it was a whole different ball game. Mick was a big man with a big personality. He seemed massive to me and quite scary. You did things how he wanted them done. If you didn't like it you could go somewhere else. The first thing you notice about Mick is how much he talks. But when it comes to training, he doesn't say much. It was serious stuff. If you messed about, he would chuck you out. Manners, and treating people properly, respectfully, were a massive thing for Mick. When you boxed, you were representing not just yourself, but your sport, your club, your trainer, your family, your town, your country, the human race, in more or less that order. He was fanatical about it.

There was another reason. Mick knew that amateur boxing was not just about the boxing. It was political. It was important to create the right impression. At every tournament we went to, Mick would have us say good morning, sir, good evening, sir, to any person wearing a badge. If you do that, he said, and all the others ignore the officials, spit on the floor as they walk past them, muttering about grey-haired old buggers, we would get the vote in a tight contest. No one spoke out of turn with Mick. We all behaved ourselves. There were some rough lads in Mick's gym. They might have needed knocking into shape when they started. When they left, they knew their manners. It was a great lesson for life, not just boxing.

I didn't know anyone when I started there. Everyone was new to me. I was a bit shy. After a few sessions Mick took me to one side and said, if you lose that puppy fat, and do what I tell you, I'll make you a champion. He was as good as his word. I kept my side of the bargain, shed half a stone. He kept his. As I progressed, the training became harder, and so did the fights. Unless you were serious about it you would never have stuck it. That's what happened to a few of my mates. They would come down a couple of times, then you would never see them again. When they came through the doors for the first time they were all like me, they wanted to be world champions. No chance. By the time I was thirteen or fourteen I was the only one doing it. I never wavered. I wasn't allowed to. My family were right behind me. If my dad couldn't make it, one of my uncles would, encouraging me, supporting me. There were a couple of other Asian kids in the gym but I was the youngest. I was also the most determined. Once I have set my heart on something that's it. I don't give up. Mick said he would make me a champion. That was good enough for me. I believed him. Let's get on with it then. That has always been my attitude. I'm greedy, hungry like that. You have to be to get on.

Outside of the gym I was a different person. In school I had grown into a model pupil. The teachers loved me. I turned up, did my work, never gave them any trouble. I left with six GCSEs. Because of the boxing I did not really have any best mates at school. The gloves were my best friends. Boxing dominated my life – training, preparing for big fights. The other kids all thought it was cool. No one ever messed with me. I was seen as the hardest lad in the school, but I never had to prove it in the yard. I did not have one fight at school. I was a peacemaker. Me, a boxer. I would say to people, what are you doing, fighting? Don't be stupid. That would be it. Trouble over.

My cousins were basically the kids I was closest to. We were just thrown together, always in each other's houses. It was habit as much as anything. There were loads of us, so it worked out great. I used to play cricket with Sajid. I wasn't big time into it. Saj was brilliant, miles better than the rest of us. He's regarded as a bowler at Lancashire, but when we were kids we could never get him out. He never gets a chance to bat at Lancs. They need to put him higher up the order. He's more of an all-rounder. Freddie Flintoff loves him. Watch out for his bother, too. Rakeb. He's an all-rounder. Couldn't get him out either. Very, very good. Rakeb has already had trials with Lancashire U-18s last year, but broke his ankle. He'll be back.

Boxing was the only thing for me. With Mick things really started to take off. But not before an early blip. I won my first fight for Bury ABC against a kid called Dean Halsall in November 1998. At least that stopped the rot. But for the next fight, the rematch with Unsworth, Mick couldn't make it. He worked shifts in a factory. He's still there now. I went with Mick's deputy, Dave Macdonald. When you are starting off, you often come up against the same people. You tend to box in your own area, so that narrows down the opponents. It was much closer this time. My dad reckoned I won the fight. The judges didn't. Mick wasn't that fussed about the result. He was more bothered about missing the fight than me losing it.

After that my boxing went to another level. There were a few good kids in the gym. They had the ability to go a long way. But on its own talent is never enough. You have to want it. You have to make sacrifices. Boxing is not an easy sport. I always had something to aim for. I wanted to fight every five minutes. Mick looked after me brilliantly. He would try to get me a fight every two weeks. There was always at least one a month. I never took the easy route. I would take on anybody. I won my next seventeen fights, going unbeaten from January 1999 to March 2000.

The pick was the fight against a lad called Clark in December. Clark was a national champion. He had a big reputation. I stopped him. That really impressed people. That run was amazing really, because club shows are a bit of a lottery, as I found out in my twenty-sixth fight against a kid called Adam King. The only person in the hall who thought I'd lost was the official who scored it for him, the only one that mattered. Even King's coach apologised. Amir, he said, I don't know what happened there. Mick went over to the official in charge. He was from Blackburn. I'm sorry, Mick said, but you don't know what you are doing. For Mick to protest like that it must have been a shocking decision. I was in tears. It was one of only two defeats I suffered with Mick in my corner. It had reached a point where it was difficult to match me. Kids started to avoid me. They would either put weight on or lose it to get into a different division.

That's when I started to think I could really make something of this. I just wanted to be the best, to achieve something that no one else had. Watching the videos of Ali started to take on a different purpose. Boxing became more than a hobby. Ambition grew into something more concrete. I wanted to be a star, too. The training made me fit and strong. Winning boosted my confidence. I felt unbeatable. Every time I won a medal or a trophy, I would get a mention in the local paper, and at school in assembly. It became a massive part of my identity. Amir Khan, boxer. That was me.

I fought for my first schoolboy title at thirteen against a lad called Bobby Ward from the famous Repton Club in London. Six weeks earlier I had fought him in Liverpool. Repton were against a Liverpool select side. I was chuffed to be invited. Ward was from a travelling family. They liked to have a bet on his fights. One bloke put £2,000 on Ward to beat me. He lost his money that night. The second fight with Ward was my first major national championships. I made it to the final. I was confident. I trained hard for the fight and felt I could handle him again. It was a close fight, not much in it. Ward got the decision. I was gutted. Losing wasn't part of my make-up. I did not expect it. I wasn't used to it. I was shocked. I wanted that title. I wanted to be under-thirteen champion of England.

I didn't dwell on it. My way of coping with setbacks was to work harder. It just made me even more determined to win next time. A year later I returned to win the junior title. From there I went on to win national titles at every level. In fact I never lost another amateur fight in England after that defeat to Ward. No one in England could test me. I beat every boxer out there. Shows would start at one in the afternoon and finish at six. Parents of other boxers used to stay behind to watch me fight. I was becoming a big star in amateur circles. They would video my fights so that their kids would be able to watch to try to pick up bits and pieces. When I was about fourteen I went to Old Trafford to watch the England-versus-Russia fight. There were a few pros from the Manchester scene who had come to watch, Ensley Bingham, who had fought for a world title, and Ricky Hatton, who was becoming a big star, were there. I had a programme and got autographs of them and I told Ricky to watch out for me. Then Ricky said to me, tell you what, Amir, why don't you give me your signature so that when you make it big, I can tell everybody that I have met you. It was mad. Pros making a fuss of me.

As an amateur it means a lot when pros talk to you, a bit like the stars at Manchester United talking to the reserves or youth team. It makes you feel good. Around the same time I did a project at school on Naseem Hamed. I wrote to him. I don't think he got it. If he did, he didn't send anything back. That really disappointed me. I stopped liking him after that. We are mates again now, but I have never forgotten. I could never do that. If anybody writes to me, I always make sure they get a reply. I get letters from everywhere. Every single one gets a response. In restaurants or hotels, when people see me, ask for an autograph or a picture, I respond. Even if I'm tired, I smile. I know how it felt to be rejected. As a kid that's not nice. You take it really personally.

I even smile at the abuse. You get some people who shout, Khan, you are rubbish. Stuff like that. I just smile, and move on. I've learned that you can't please everybody.

Dealing with fame was never an issue before the Olympics. I was known only in amateur boxing circles. It was funny how quickly things changed. When I first started competing properly, Taz would inform the local paper in Bolton. He would send an email to a man called David Magilton on the *Evening News* Sports Desk with bullet points confirming my age, the date, time, venue and the result. By the time I was thirteen, the paper was calling us. I have news clips from when I was eight years old all the way to the Olympics. My first was when the local paper took a picture of the gym at the Halliwell Club in Bolton. I was at the end of the line, just sneaked into view. I used to cut them all out. Now I'm in the papers every day, or at least that's how it feels. I do not have the time to keep up my cuttings file. It was exciting when it started. To see your picture in the paper for the first time was mad. Incredibly, I never fought in Bolton as an amateur, apart from the Kindelan fight before I turned pro. I was always fighting in my opponents' back yards.

One year, in the space of six months I won three national titles: the national schoolboys, the national boys' clubs and the junior ABA. I don't think that had ever been done before. They could not keep me out of the ring. I've even fought at two hours' notice. We just loaded up the car and set off. That is what it was like in those days. We were a team. The family would jump in and off we would go all over the country. They were mostly dinner shows. Brilliant it was.

My first international appearance was in Ipswich. I was fighting a Scottish kid at 48 kilos. Again I was the only Asian lad at the tournament. Pin thin I was then. All the fat had gone. I burned it off running when I got home from school and doing millions of sit-ups before bed. He thought it was going to be easy. Most of them did before they knew who I was. I boxed his ears off. I won best boxer on my debut for England. I felt like I could walk back to Bolton. On the way home I kept going through reruns of the night, walking out first, the announcer's voice, Amir Khan representing England at 48 kilos. That was a massive thing for me. There were a lot of kids in England boxing at my weight. Out of all of them the ABA chose me. My confidence started to go through the roof. I was like the Wayne Rooney of amateur boxing. My style, my background, it was all pretty unique. I was doing things in a way that had not really been done before by a lad of my background. People saw the Asian thing and made a big fuss about it. For me and my family, it was only ever about Amir Khan. For others it seemed to be important for different reasons, reasons that would become more obvious to me after the Olympics when young Asians from similar Pakistani backgrounds disappeared into London tube stations and on buses with bombs hidden in rucksacks.

The only time I ever had a problem was at a show in Preston. I was fighting a lad called Bowker from the Northside Club in Clayton, Manchester. He was a really nice lad. It was the Greater Manchester Finals, January 2002. I was fifteen. By then I had built quite a big reputation in the amateurs. When I boxed in competitions the other lads knew that I was the one they had to beat. Northside is a big amateur club. They have a massive following. The venue was packed and as usual many people had travelled to Preston from Clayton. There was a lot of shouting and cheering going on when we entered the ring.

I started to get the upper hand. I won the first round. It was the same story in the second. The Northside supporters were starting to get a bit frustrated. One lad jumped on to the apron at the side of the ring and started shouting and pointing at me. It looked at one point as though he was trying to get in the ring. There was real hate in his face. No one is allowed anywhere near the apron except officials and corners. The referee immediately stopped the fight whilst they got the guy away from ringside. I had never experienced anything like that in my career. Mick was furious. The contest restarted. In the third and final round I had Bowker backed into the corner where his supporters were gathered. One of them spat on my leg. I couldn't believe it. I stopped fighting and held my arms wide apart as if to say to the ref, what is going on? I won the fight easily.

Afterwards Mick and my dad complained to the ABA. I'm not convinced it was totally about race. It was more about the fact that I was battering the lad. They didn't like it. There is a lot of local rivalry at that level. The Northside crowd had been building up to this fight. Maybe race came into it after that. Either way it wasn't a nice thing to have to deal with. My dad and uncles were really upset about it. Boxing is obviously a violent sport. Emotions run high. But there is never any hostility outside the ring. The amateurs are really hot on that stuff. The Northside Club coach came into the changing room afterwards and apologised. So did Bowker. It wasn't his fault. I felt sorry for the lad that he had been put in that position. A couple of months after it happened we met up in Blackpool. We are still mates now.

A year later at the same venue in the same competition, I fought another kid from Northside. He was supposed to be a tough lad, a judo champion. I stopped him. Again it was noisy at ringside, but nowhere near as bad as the year before.

Fighting for England made a huge difference to me. I was no longer a lad fighting on local bills. I was a proper boxer now. I was treated with a lot of respect within the sport. My reputation spread. Basically I did what came naturally. I might have made things look easy but really there was a lot of hard work that went into it. I was fit as a fiddle. I had loads of stamina. I was so fit I captained the school athletics team as well. Once, the school wanted me to run at a county athletics event. I won a Bolton schools 1,500 metres event by a distance. They wanted me to compete in Greater Manchester. After that it would have been the nationals. I couldn't because I had a boxing match on the same day. The teachers were disappointed. I remember Mr Dickinson telling the school I could represent the country at running as well as boxing. It was a bit embarrassing really, listening to a teacher say that in front of 400 other lads. The school saw me as a role model.

My stamina meant that my punch rate was so high opponents used to give up in the end. I was dedicated and had a brilliant coach. Mick was fantastic at letting kids develop at their own pace in their own style. He would teach them the basics, make sure they understood the fundamentals but would never try to make you something you were not.

A lot of it comes down to nature, the body you were born with. Boxers tend to fall into types depending on their body shape. Short, stocky lads tend to be scrappers, like I was when I started out. Taller kids with longer reaches tend to adopt different styles, jab and move. I was a bit unusual because I shot up in my early teens. I changed from a flat-footed slugger to a boxer known more for speed and movement. The thing that stayed with me was my fighting instinct. I love the physical aspect of the sport, throwing punches, getting stuck in. That's what got me started and what keeps me at it.

Mick recognised this and let me off the leash. His training sessions were hard, but enjoyable. Without people like Mick amateur boxing would not survive. They give their time for nothing. Thousands of kids passed through the gym, all of them enjoying the thrill of the sport, hitting the pads, the bags, pulling on gloves for the first time. Trainers and coaches hope that one day a champion will walk through the door. Mick spotted something in me straight away. But it is a two-way thing. If I had not found him, and Bury ABC, things might have turned out differently for me, and Mick would not have had his champion. He tells people that I was his Red Rum, a freak event that happens once in a generation. But I know I was lucky to have him, too. He is still an important part of my boxing life, though he no longer trains me.

Mick is working with my younger brother Haroon. I think Mick wishes Haroon had my attitude to training. If Mick said run a mile, I would run two. I would train 24/7 if I could. Haroon would miss training 24/7 if he could get away with it. His mentality is totally different. He's probably more talented than me. He is still winning easily. If he trained as hard as I did at that age no one would touch him. People have got him down for a medal at the London Olympics in 2012. He'll be twenty. He's already boxed for England. It is easy at that stage to get carried away. Your confidence soars. But I learned from experience. After my first three amateur fights my confidence was so high I thought I was unbeatable. I learned that you can never be fit enough, that you have to prepare like a challenger in every fight, even when you are a champion. When I lost the next three fights I went back to the gym and worked harder. I never lost confidence. I always believed in myself because I knew how much effort I had put in.

People seemed to like it. I was a ticket seller even then. We always had problems getting enough tickets for the family at shows. They were mostly dinner shows and all banged out. Each boxer would be allocated two tickets for family members. We could have sold ten, twenty times that number easily. Tickets were eventually at the centre of the big row with the ABA at the end of my amateur career. It was a major factor in my decision to turn pro. Before I reached that point there was a big adventure waiting to happen that came completely out of the blue. And all because the ABA wouldn't send me to the World Cadet Championships in 2003. If they had done, I might never have gone to Athens in 2004. I was sixteen. The ABA reckoned I was not old enough to compete. Mick argued the case, but they wouldn't have it. I was gutted. I was the outstanding candidate. I could not have done more domestically or for England. Instead they sent me off to the Junior Olympics in America. It might have sounded grand but it was nowhere near as important as the World Cadets. In the end it turned out to be more important than anybody could have imagined.

2

Athens Calling

By the time I arrived in Louisiana for the Junior Olympics in July 2003 I was over my disappointment and determined to prove to the ABA that I should have gone to the Cadets. When I left three fights later holding the gold medal and the award for best boxer, my head was spinning with possibilities. And not just because I was leaving as a champion. I beat the American no. 1, Victor Ortiz, in the final. Stopped him. Ortiz was a class kid. He was highly regarded by everybody, not just the Americans. He just could not adapt to my style. I was too quick for him. I caught him with some clean shots, clean enough to give him standing counts three times. Three of them and you are out. The referee had no choice. When he indicated the bout was over it was the sweetest feeling.

In the first round I stopped a Puerto Rican lad. In the second I stopped the American no. 2. And now in the final I had done it again to the favourite for gold. No English kid had ever done that before. My dad was so proud, smiling from ear to ear. The Americans were all over me afterwards. They wanted to know if I was going to Athens. I said no. It had never crossed my mind. We didn't think I was old enough. The Americans could not believe it. In England you are not allowed to box at senior ABA champion-ships until you are eighteen. Under Olympic rules you can box at senior level when you arc seventeen. When the Americans worked out that I would meet the age criterion they offered me the chance to represent them. They were deadly serious. They went through the whole process with me. They said they would arrange a green card for me. Everything. That would be it. Amir Khan, a Yank. I could have won silver for the Stars and Stripes.

It was a non-starter for me. Unthinkable. How could I, a boy from Bolton, fight in an American vest? But it did set my mind racing. I had always planned to fight at the Olympics. Never in my wildest dreams did I believe it would be in Athens. Beijing was the target. Now the idea of going to Greece was in my head. The problem was, it was not in the heads of the ABA. On the way back from America my dad spoke to Ian Irwin, the ABA performance director. What about Amir fighting at the Olympics, Ian? He'd like to give it a go. The reply was forthright, and delivered in a way that told me it should end there. Out of the question, he said. He is too young. They are men in there. He is a baby. My dad shrugged. He took things on trust. If you tell my dad something, his instinct is to believe you. If he finds out later that a betrayal has taken place then he is a different man. He thought there must have been a misunderstanding in America. Maybe Amir was too young after all. I was not convinced. I did some homework on the internet when I got back. The Americans were right. I was eligible to fight in Athens.

The European Cadet Championships were coming up. Bar the Cubans and Americans, the best under-16s in the world would be there. I needed to do well to make the ABA think again. I walked through them. Five fights. Nearly stopped all of my opponents and won the best boxer award. After that we sat down with Ian and laid our cards on the table. I needed a tougher test. I wanted to go to the Olympics.

The ABA was still far from convinced. There was a lot of debate about it. Ian spoke to Terry Edwards. Terry was a coach with the senior England squad. He had seen me box three or four times in the juniors and heard good things about me. Terry was in Liverpool with the senior team when Ian called him. What do you think, Terry, should we bring him in? Terry said that if I was as good as the reports suggested then we had to. Good old Terry. He did not know me personally but was instinctively on my side. He has never left it. They decided to send me to the European Schoolboys Championships in Italy, a tournament for under-17s and a much tougher test. If I lost there, forget it. The pressure was on. I had to win. Competition is the element I have always loved best. The harder the challenge, the higher I climb to meet it. I stopped everyone. Again I was voted the tournament's best boxer.

Still the ABA officials dragged their feet. It wasn't Terry. He was very supportive. He was in the hands of the ABA every bit as much as I was. It was killing me. We remembered what the Americans had said. We knew we could not fight for them, but there was another possibility. Like my grandfather, my dad was also born in Matore, a small village near Rawalpindi, in the north of Pakistan. Making the necessary arrangements would not be difficult if we had to. I'm English through and through, but I was desperate. If I had to wear the colours of my ancestors, then so be it.

We went back to the ABA. When they again said no, my dad played the trump card. It was a risk because once a decision like that is made, there is no turning back. I wanted to fight under the Union Jack. I knew I was ready. I had done all I could to show them that. As far as we were concerned, the ABA was not being fair to me. Under the circumstances we felt justified in applying pressure. Time was running out. It was November 2003. I would turn seventeen on 8 December. There was a major tournament coming up in January. The Olympic qualifiers would follow in March. It had to be now. At the last minute, the ABA relented. They would send me to a senior training camp in Sheffield in December to determine my fitness and suitability.

I had only ever sparred with kids my own age. Once you step

up to senior level you are in with men, proper, big blokes. The no. 1 at 60 kilos was twenty-six. Terry sat me down. It was our first real meeting. He outlined his concerns, tried to explain the difference between fighting someone my own age and sharing a ring with a fully grown man. In my age group, opponents would not exactly run away, but they didn't always provide the stiffest test. In this company, when blokes got hit, they stood their ground. Not only that, they would hit you back. And harder. I was still a schoolboy, a student at college in Bolton. I could tell Terry was a bit worried. He spoke about tactics, about movement and the need to alter one or two things. The sparring was full on. Terry needn't have worried. I found it easy. I was catching my sparring partner with so many shots, I felt great. I kept up with the training no problem; running, weights, the lot. The only thing that freaked me was the ice baths. I had never heard of an ice bath before. Terry had all the fighters doing four one-minute blasts. I did not fancy it one bit. In I went. Fifteen seconds later I was out. I could not stand it. Terry explained the benefits. Gradually he coaxed me back in. By the time I got to the Olympics I was having an ice bath every day. It's brilliant for getting rid of toxins and promoting recovery.

Terry was impressed. On the Sunday night he and I went for a walk to kill a bit of time. There was a big Mercedes showroom opposite. Terry took a shine to one model, a CL500 I think, worth a fiver short of £150,000. If you win gold at the Olympics you can buy me that, he said. If you win a medal I'll stop smoking. He reckons I settled for silver so I didn't have to pay out on the bet. He stopped smoking though.

After Sheffield, the ABA had to find me a senior competition. I was not old enough to fight under ABA rules in England. There was a tournament coming up in Germany, the Adidas Boxing Gala. The ABA sent a full team. Every boxer would fight three bouts, win or lose. I was the only English lad to win all three. It was hard. We went out two weeks before. We were training with the Germans and the French. I sparred with the world no. 2. I was catching him. I could see him getting frustrated. He is a good mate of mine now, Vitali Tiber. He was the German captain, the best boxer there. I made him look stupid in front of his mates and his team. It gave me massive confidence.

The first fight was tough. A proper man he was. About twenty-four or twenty-five, and strong with it. He caught me with a good shot. My legs were going. I had been caught before in sparring but not like this. I knew I had to recover. I was given my first standing count as a senior. It taught me an important lesson. Keep your hands up. After three rounds I was knackered. I got back to the corner and stood up, expecting Terry to take off my head guard and get the gloves off. Sit down, son, said Terry. You have got another round. I had only done three-rounders before that. I didn't know. It was a great learning experience. I went back out. He caught me again but nothing great. In the end I beat him by ten points. That impressed the ABA.

The next fight was at a different venue in another town. Again it was against a German lad, a world bronze medallist. I watched videos of him with Terry the night before. After the first fight I kept my hands high. It worked. I went out and stopped him in the second round. The place went berserk.

The next day, before the third fight, my dad was approached by a German promoter, a representative of Universum, massive players in Germany. He had made the trip especially to see me. Word had got around Germany that there was this English kid pulling up trees. He wanted to speak to me after the tournament. The English coaches and team manager saw what was happening. They told me to keep away from Universum. Don't go near those guys. I went out and beat the German no. 3 in my last fight by more than twenty points. Again I was voted best boxer. That brought Universum straight back.

I kept in the background and let Dad do the talking. It would not hurt to listen to what they had to say. They wanted me to go to Germany to see their headquarters and the facilities they provided for their boxers. Over there the amateurs and pros work together. Universum had a few amateurs going to the Olympics. They wanted me to be part of their team. In the end we settled on a meeting in Manchester at the airport. It was all very flattering. At the time not many people knew about me outside of the England camp. No one had approached us before. He threw some impressive figures at us. My dad had a scrapyard in Bolton. He was doing all right. We were comfortable but no more than that. The money would have made a big difference. Silly money, as Mick Jelley, my coach at Bury ABC, described it. And at that point I had not even qualified for the Olympics. They offered two deals, one contract if I made it to the Olympics, another if I won a medal. Either one would have made me a rich boy. We declined. My dad reckoned that if the Germans were prepared to offer big money at this stage, there would be better deals to consider down the line. As usual he was right. But it was nice to know people were interested.

The real benefit was in the ring. I had forced my way into contention. The ABA now had a choice to make: to take the ABA champion at 60 kilos, Stephen Burke, or me. I was ready to go into a box-off to decide. It didn't come to that. They chose me. I didn't really know Stephen, but I had sparred with him at the training camp in Sheffield. I felt for him. But there is no room for sentiment in sport. You have to be a bit greedy to get on. I got what I wanted. Now for the real test, the Olympic qualifiers.

The first one was in Croatia. The European qualifiers are the hardest in the world to win. Since the break-up of the Soviet Union, there are far more boxers from places like Kazakhstan, Georgia, Uzbekistan, etc. all competing where once there would have been just one Soviet fighter in my weight category. I was shocked at the size of them. Compared to us, the Europeans looked massive, all fully grown men. I was the youngest, baby-faced. I don't think I had even had a shave by then.

The draw was made. I drew a Georgian lad. I did not know a thing about him. He was big, facial hair, ripped body, hairy arms. You could see he was a hard bloke, that he'd had a tough life. He was easily ten years older than me. When he drew me out of the hat he thought he was on to a winner straight away. In amateur boxing no one has much respect for English fighters. They look at us and think it will be an easy fight. That gave me a mental edge. It's that competitive thing again. It has always been inside me. I love to fight.

I was catching him but not scoring. The whole bout went like that. I thought I did enough to win. So did Terry. The judges thought differently and gave him the decision. I was gutted. It was my first defeat in four years. That night I watched the video. I still could not see how the officials scored me the loser. I was not the only one to taste defeat. No English lads got through. The coaches sympathised. I told them not to worry. If I met him again I would beat him. We came back home, watched the video over and over, then prepared for the next qualifier in Bulgaria.

I got my fitness back up. Terry was very keen on that. He wanted to improve my strength and conditioning. After junior tournaments I felt like I could get in the ring straight away and do it all again. Fighting in the seniors was a different game. I needed to be stronger than I had ever been and fitter. There wasn't much time to work on technical things. It was more about becoming more tactically aware. Everything Terry said I took in like a sponge. I think he was impressed by my attitude and the speed at which I picked things up. It didn't seem difficult to me. I loved what I was doing. Terry put me through a punishing training cycle. I did all my running, practised fighting against different styles, then flew out to Plovdiv.

When the draw was made I drew the same bloke. The hairy fella from Georgia. Unbelievable. I wasn't bothered because I felt I beat him the first time. I was glad in a way because it gave me the chance to prove a point to the judges and officials. The

Me aged six months with Grandma Iqbal Begum

Dad and Mum

Aged twelve months getting up to mischief with my elder sister Tabinda

My cousin Khalid, Tabinda, Mum, me and Rosemana at my second birthday party

About to start
nursery aged four,
with my front teeth
missing

Visiting Father
Christmas with
Tabinda in Bolton
Shopping Centre

Visiting Pakistan
(top, left to right): Tabinda, Sabia, Haroon and me
(bottom, left to right): Haroon, Mum, me, Dad and Tabinda

Auntie Shiraz, Dad, Grandad Lall Khan, Grandma Iqbal Begum,
Uncle Shahid (Terry) and Auntie Shanaz in 1970

Uncle Terry,
Grandma, Dad
and seven-year-
old Uncle Tahir
(Taz) in 1978

Posing with my first pair of boxing gloves

Winning my first trophy, for Best Newcomer,
at Bolton Lads & Girls Club, aged eleven

Showing off a few
more trophies with
my cousin Hassan and
brother Haroon

A snap from my first fight (and first win!)
at Stoke-on-Trent, vs M. Jones from Atherstone . . .

. . . and winning my last Schoolboy Championships
in 1993, with Mick Jelley (left) and my dad (right)

former Eastern bloc countries have a lot of influence in the European amateurs. I knew I had to be ready. Out came the video of the first fight again. I pored over it with Terry. We were building a really strong relationship now.

Terry was an experienced coach. He had done five world championships, three Commonwealth Games, two Olympics. He had been in this situation before, taking over kids who had spent most of their amateur careers working with one coach. He spoke to my family a lot, to my dad and Taz. He included Mick in preparations. There were always many discussions in the training camp environment. That helped a lot. Dad appreciated that because he knew how much it affected me having a different coach in the corner. Like Mick, Terry didn't try to change too much. He recognised my strengths. I was a quick learner, I had quick hands and feet, a decent internal radar that allowed me to judge distance well. And I read a fight pretty well.

The next day when I went to the venue, I warmed up and felt sharp. The bell went and I boxed the ears off the lad. He did not know where the punches were coming from. In the third round I was nineteen points up, just one point from forcing a stoppage. He made it to the fourth, just. In the last round the stoppage rule on points does not apply. I ended up winning by twenty-five points. It felt no different from the first fight. This time I got the decision.

In the next round I drew an Armenian. Another tough fight. Mick was out with us. Not in my corner. More for moral support. But as always he had plenty of input. Mick had seen this lad in the first round against a Swedish boxer. He beat the Swede up badly. Compared to me he was dead old, pushing thirty. This was the kind of test the ABA was concerned about, a fight against a mature man. It was made even harder because for the Armenians and Georgians it was the last qualifying opportunity. Lose in Bulgaria and no Olympics.

The Armenians were always terrific fighters. He was punch perfect, fast hands, great footwork and a southpaw to boot.

Mick came up to me and said, Amir, this is going to be a tough fight. I was a little nervous. But that was good. It gives you snap. I had another advantage. Surprise. I was young. I could tell he was looking at me as this scrawny English kid. Who does he think he is? he thought. To be fair to him I was dead skinny, no muscle, no definition on my arms. He thought I was easy meat. You couldn't blame him. He came charging out of his corner like a bull out of a gate. As he came into range I whacked him with a left hook. Bang. That one punch sorted him out for the fight. I could see he was hurt. His eyes had gone. He was dead strong, massive legs. He didn't fall, but he was gone. I kept the pressure on, kept making him miss. I stopped him in the third round, twenty points clear. To stop someone like him was a massive thing, a real statement. After that I felt I had the judges on my side. The officials all wanted to shake my hand. They started saying I could go to the Olympics and win a medal. One more win and I would be there.

I was drawn against a Romanian. If Mick was worried about the Armenian, he was double-worried about this opponent. Mick, as always, had videoed his previous fight, against a Russian. He sat down and watched it with my dad. Mick always looks serious. He's just got one of those faces. The look on his face when he asked my dad what he thought told me he was very serious. You'd have thought I was fighting King Kong. You know me, Shah, I always tell the truth, he said. This fella looks like he is going to win the gold medal to me. Mick watched the video three times. He could not see a flaw. You are going to have to pull something out of the bag to beat him, Mick said. Thanks, Mick. No pressure there then. Let me have a little think, said Mick. Off he went to mull it over. A couple of hours later he was walking with my dad. He shouted, I've got it. My dad didn't know what he was talking about. You've got what, Mick? The answer. What is it? Hit him with the hardest punch you have thrown in your life. Brilliant, Mick, you're a genius. He was, too.

We had spent so much time concentrating on the Romanian's strengths on the video, we nearly missed an obvious point. Though it was a tear-up with the Russian, the Romanian bossed the fight, dictated the rhythm of the bout. In that sense he was never under any real pressure. The fight went the way he wanted it to. I wouldn't allow him the same luxury.

At the European Junior Championships he had stopped Frankie Gavin in the second round. Frankie won gold at the Commonwealths in Melbourne. He's a cracking boxer. That tells you how good this Romanian lad was. He was thirty-two, almost double my age. He was absolutely at the top of his game.

In the changing room beforehand everyone was dead quiet. All the other English lads had been knocked out of the competition. There was only me left. I was on my own just thinking about the fight. The coaches were more nervous than me. They were making me nervous. Nobody was talking to me. Then, as I made my way to the ring, loads of little kids kept coming up to me, shaking my hand, saying my name. The officials were nodding at me. I had boxed so well in the first two bouts my reputation had spread.

Everybody recognised me, including the Romanian. He never took a backwards step. It was like he was glued to me. He had definitely done his homework, too. I was like a marked man in football. I don't think I have ever thrown as many shots in a fight. The first one was a good one, a big right hand, just as Mick advised. It earned me the Romanian's respect. At the end of the third round I was leading by ten points. One round away from the Olympic Games. I was also dead on my feet. That last round was the hardest of my career so far. The whole fight was. He would not stay off me. I was tasting blood. Still he kept coming, throwing punches, working my body. It was all or nothing for him. He wanted it badly. I managed to land a few big punches to stay in front. I won the fight.

The coaches went mad. Everybody went mad. I had qualified. I was going to Athens. Everybody else had lost. I was the youngest boxer in the tournament, one of the youngest to qualify for the Olympics. It was a brilliant feeling. My mind flashed back to the times that people had said I was too young, had tried to persuade me not to go, thought I was a baby, thought I would get beat up against all these big, bad men. I remember warming up outside in Italy at the student tournament before Christmas and the coach Jim Davidson coming up to me, trying to tell me to forget about the seniors. Stay with me in the juniors, he said. I'll look after you. When I qualified I shut a lot of people up. I did it in good style, too.

Mick went up to the Romanian afterwards. He had a tear in his eye. Mick had been in the game a long while, seen a lot of boxers come and go, knew what it meant to senior amateurs at this stage of their careers. The Romanian was one of the best Mick had seen. He knew he would never have another chance to fight at the Olympics. When Mick went up it was one genuine boxing man paying his respects to another.

I did not have to fight in the final because my opponent, an Azerbaijani boxer, pulled out. So I won gold and picked up yet another best boxer trophy.

The papers went mad. I came home to loads of local media attention, interview after interview. I wasn't used to it. I was dead shy, so bad at it. I couldn't even talk properly. I stuttered a lot, bumbled through really. It didn't matter. Everyone loved Amir Khan. I thought wow, if it is like this now, what will it be like if I win a medal at the Olympics? I wasn't complaining. I signed my first commercial deal with Adidas. It was just for the Olympic period. They gave me lots of kit and stuff. I loved it. They were the main sponsors for the Olympic Games and they were making a fuss of me. I was so proud. Overnight I became a celebrity in Bolton. I was used to people in boxing knowing about me. But this was different. Strangers would come up to me to wish me well for the Olympics. I enjoyed the moment. Chilled out a bit, then started to focus.

There was a pre-Olympic tournament in Athens. Things were set out just as they would be at the Games to give boxers a feeling of what to expect. Everybody would be there. I was really looking forward to it, checking out the boxers who I would be fighting for real a few weeks later. But Terry wasn't up for it. He didn't want me to go. He couldn't see the point of letting boxers who might be fighting me get a look close up. I was still an unknown quantity to most of the seniors. I had had only a handful of senior fights. He thought I would be giving away an advantage, one that might come in very handy at the Olympics.

Terry was outvoted. I was on my way. Great, I thought. Let me at them. I didn't care who knew about me. I just wanted to fight. There was only one boxer I wanted to avoid, and that was the Cuban legend Mario Kindelan, Olympic champion in 2000 and favourite to win in Athens in my class.

I was travelling back from a training session on the bus. The draw had been made. I had no idea who I was fighting. Then a Pakistani lad told me I was up against a Cuban. It could only have been Kindelan. Great. I'm fighting the best amateur boxer in the world at any weight first up. How lucky is that? I tried to stay positive. The coaches were dead quiet but I thought, hey, better fight him now so that if I have to box him later in the tournament I will know something about him. I was two months old when Kindelan had his first bout. He had been fighting literally all my life.

By the time the fight came around I was buzzing. Not fazed at all. I felt great. I thought I was doing well. He did not really catch me with a good shot. I was catching him all the time. I thought I was winning it. When the scores were added up I lost by twenty points. I could not believe it. I thought there must have been some mistake. There wasn't. The wonders of the electronic age and their fancy scoring systems had struck again. That was it for me at that tournament. But I learned so much. I looked at the video when I got home and thought Kindelan was beatable. I would have fought him the next day and fancied my chances. No bother. In a way I don't think Terry was too bothered either. He was pleased in a sense that I was still relatively unknown. No one would be looking out for me now.

I came home itching to get on with it. I was so keen in fact that I almost jeopardised my dream. By concentrating so much on the Olympics I had ignored the World Junior Championships that were coming up in Korea just before Athens. I desperately wanted to go. I got the crazy idea into my head that I could do both, fuelled by the fact that the ABA didn't send me to the World Cadet Championships. It hurt like mad to miss out on them. The World Juniors would never come around for me again. Terry was right behind me. He thought it would be a good idea to step down to the juniors again to rebuild rhythm and confidence for the Olympics, to shake out the aftereffects of the defeat to Kindelan.

We asked Ian Irwin. He said no. The ABA had mapped out the period before the Olympics for me. It was too much of a risk. What if I were injured, broke a bone in my hand or something? The Olympics would be out of the window. I could see their point, but I wouldn't be told. I had a bee in my bonnet about it like kids do. I reckoned the World Championships would come around again and again as a senior. So would the Olympics, for that matter. There was also another reason. I had had only seven fights at senior level. Like Terry I thought it would be good experience, good preparation for the Olympics. Ian was head of the coaching team, senior in rank to Terry but not the highest authority in amateur boxing. We asked if there was anyone else we could speak to. Ian said he would talk it through with team selector, Keith Walters, on my behalf. The next day he called back to say he had spoken to Keith and the answer was still no.

I took it badly. I was perhaps getting things out of proportion. I was headstrong, full of confidence and thought I could rule the world. The Worlds were only two days away now. The Olympics were still six weeks down the line. At that point I could not see beyond Korea. I dug in. My dad phoned Keith direct and told him that if a choice had to be made I would rather go to the Worlds. Keith was stunned. He could not believe that after all I had gone through to get to Athens I was prepared to sacrifice the Olympics this time around. It did not make sense. Keith asked for a day to think about it. He phoned Ian that night. They talked it through at length. The next day he called back. You can do both, he said. Yes! A result!

I flew out to Korea almost immediately. I knew all the juniors from international cadet tournaments. We mixed with all the fighters from other countries, shared the facilities. You try to have a bit of banter in tournament situations. When I told the lads from Kazakhstan what weight category I was in they laughed and said I was going to get beaten up. The English lads came straight back at them, told them I was going to the Olympics. They thought we were mad.

When it came to the weigh-in I thought the officials were mad. I stood on the scales, made the weight, then I was told that I had to come back when I'd had a shave. The coaches laughed. A shave? Baby-faced Amir, shave? You can get a cat to lick that off. There were a few wispy bits of bum fluff on my chin. Nothing really. But they made such a fuss I had to get rid of it and come back.

When the draw was made the lads were pulling my leg, saying that I would probably get an easy draw. They would get the Kazakhs, the Uzbeks, Amir, the superstar on his way to the Olympic Games, would get the lad from Taipei. That's what happened. Amazingly I got the lad from Taipei. I didn't even know they boxed in that country. I stopped him in the second round. I came back at the end of the first round eighteen points up. I got a slap from the coach, Chris Edmunds. What are you playing at? You've got to get him out of the ring. The lad is hopeless, he can't fight. Get him out of there. I was too frightened to fail. I went straight out, hit him with two more shots and stopped him. The only shot I took was from Chris.

In the second round I was paired with a lad called Jorge Hernandez, the World Cadet Champion, cousin of the great Mario Kindelan, and the latest in a long line of fighters from one of Cuba's great boxing dynasties. All the Irish lads had seen him box. He fought a bit like me, they said, only better. They thought he would beat me. There was massive interest in the fight. In the end it turned out to be one of my easiest bouts. I caught him with a body shot early. I could see he didn't know where he was. He kept looking at his corner. It was obvious he did not know what to do. The referee gave him two standing counts in the fight. I have never seen a Cuban in such distress. Even our team manager could not believe it. Amir has just beaten up a Cuban like he was a normal boxer. All the officials came up offering congratulations, saying I would win best boxer at the tournament. It was only the second bout. I was buzzing.

Then disaster. My right hand started killing me. I couldn't make a fist. I didn't feel anything in the excitement of the fight. As things calmed down, afterwards, the pain started to come through. I had clipped Hernandez in the second round, a right hook to the head. I caught him awkwardly with my thumb. Afterwards my hand swelled, turned black and blue. I was sure I had fractured something.

Peter Hayes, the team manager, said that was it. He was taking me out of the competition. The Olympics, barely a month away, were now in serious doubt. There were a lot of I told you sos flying around. This is why we did not want you to come, etc. I was headstrong. I had just beaten the best lad in the competition. I reckoned I could beat the rest one-handed. I probably wasn't thinking straight. I was in the sweet shop. I wanted everything, the more so because I knew what was possible.

I went to see the physio, Carolyn. She established there was no fracture. Great news. She iced it, gave me some gentle massage and treatment. She was brilliant. A genius. The hand was still painful but I got my way. They decided I would box on.

Next up was a Kazakh lad, the same one who was laughing at me when we arrived, giving it the big one. You are not going to the Olympics. All that. He wasn't laughing now. People talk at international competitions. Who's the best fighter? Stuff like that. After beating up the Cuban I was the talk of the tournament. I looked across at his corner. His face was white. Scared stiff, he was. I still couldn't make a proper fist. Getting the glove on was a struggle. But he didn't know that.

I jabbed my way through the fight. I couldn't risk throwing the right. It was hard because instinctively when you get in position you want to let go with it. It's the honey punch. I still won the bout by sixteen points. The officials who had seen me outclass Hernandez were puzzled. They came up to my dad afterwards and said that I was not the same Amir Khan who had beaten the Cuban so heavily. We couldn't say anything. If the doctors knew that I was carrying an injury to my hand I would be out of the competition.

I was through to the semis now. The coaches asked once more if I wanted to pull out. The hand was still hurting. But I was determined. I went back to the hotel for more treatment with Carolyn, working tirelessly on the hand. I was up against a French lad in the semis, a good fighter. Again it was a struggle to put the glove on. The bell went. He was a lot taller than me. I walked out, threw a couple of jabs then, instinctively, threw the right hand. Bang. I sparked him. He was a tough lad, as well. No duck egg. He had beaten some good boxers. His legs went. I didn't feel a thing. I couldn't believe I had knocked him out so easily, and with my bad hand, too.

I had three days to recover before the final. In the hotel where we were staying everybody was talking about it. The fight was going out live on Korean TV. I was up against an Uzbek. The hotel staff would approach me. Tell me how good I was. Shadow box in front of me in my style. It was mad. The Koreans were so friendly. They had completely taken to me for some reason. The hand was improving by the day. I still couldn't throw a full-blooded shot. But it was OK. Good enough to batter him. I gave him two standing counts. The bell saved him in the final round. I'd won. Now I was the World Junior Champion. The trophy they gave me was massive. The feeling was even better. How confident did that make me feel? I was absolutely flying. This is what I had come for. I had showed the Cubans what I was about. Beat their best man. I was more than ready for the Olympics, now just three weeks away.

Before I went out, Asif, who is now my business manager, organised a barbecue as a going-away thing. I thought it would be a little do with a few mates. It was packed. Kids from the School Shuttle Childcare Services where I used to work turned up, loads of local media, even the TV cameras. It was crazy. I remember driving over in my mate Saj's Daewoo. Tiny thing it was. When we got there it was mobbed. It really threw me. At first I did not want to get out of the car. I was stunned to see all the reporters and TV people. It was OK in the end. I really enjoyed it.

After that it was time to put on my focus head. Though I was the only British boxer to qualify, one of the youngest to get to the Olympics, there was not too much national interest in me before the Games started. I did a bit of media stuff with the boxing press, but most of the focus was on the big track and field stars like Paula Radcliffe and Kelly Holmes, and the rowers. People like that. Though I was big news in boxing circles, boxing wasn't big news in Olympic circles. Not back home, anyway.

Because I was the only boxer going to Athens they sent out two other boxers – Neil Perkins, who was first reserve at the 69-kilo weight, and Darren Langley – to keep me company, help with the training. Usually when I travelled to an event I would be with a whole team, twelve other lads. At the pre-Olympic training camp in France I was only with Neil. Boredom was a real problem, a seventeen-year-old lad training just with one other boxer. I hated it. I had a good relationship with my coach, Terry, but I needed people around me of my own age. Having Darren and Neil around after that helped me a lot with my preparations.

In Cyprus at the pre-Olympic training camp I recognised all the other athletes, Paula and Matthew Pinsent, people like that. But they did not have a clue who I was. I would walk past all the big noises like Pinsent but I was too shy to go up to them, to ask for an autograph, or something like that. They would have thought, who is this idiot? I was starstruck.

By the time we arrived in the Olympic village in Athens, I was friendly with a few of the other athletes. I hung out a bit with badminton player Gail Emms and her doubles partner Nathan Robertson. They were really cool. We all had dinner once or twice, but it was still pretty lonely. I shared a room with a weightlifter, but he was gone after two days so then it was mostly back to me and my trainer Terry.

It helped having a lodge in the village where family and close friends could meet. It took my mind off things, allowed me to chill out. After training I would go there in the evenings to spend time with my dad and some mates from Bolton. It made a difference. Boxing was off the agenda. We never once talked about it. It was nice to hear what they had been up to. My uncle Taz had organised for fifteen friends and family to come over. Everybody bought tickets for the whole tournament. They paid about £400 each for them. I think they got their money's worth.

By the time the boxing competition started I had been in the Olympic village for two weeks. Man, I couldn't wait to get started. As long as I didn't draw Kindelan in the first round, I would settle for anyone, except maybe a Greek. Just my luck, I drew the Greek champion first up, the local favourite. In my half of the draw, if I got past the Greek, there was the European champion from Bulgaria, then the Asian champion from Korea, and a Kazakh kid in the semis. The draw could hardly have been tougher. At least I would not have to fight Kindelan until the final, if I got that far.

The Greek boxer didn't qualify. He was given a wild card. I had seen him fight. He was no mug. I was a bit nervous. Though I had fought at big championships in the six months leading up to the Games, I had not experienced anything like this. The atmosphere was electric. There was huge interest, photographers and camera crews everywhere. When I walked out into the arena you could hear a pin drop. When he walked out the place erupted. The venue held 13,000 people. There were not many spaces. It was hot, too, early afternoon. I was a little bit over-whelmed. There was a lot to take in, a lot of distractions. After the warm-up in the holding area, where the boxers gather before making their way to the ring, Terry pulled me to one side. He had worked out that to get to my corner of the ring I had to walk around the whole arena almost. Take your time, Terry said. Use that time to clear your head. This was for real, the big stage. It was sound advice. I was announced . . . and representing Great Britain, Amir Khan. I bolted out of the holding area, completely ignoring what Terry had said. My brain could not process the information. There was too much happening. Terry had to jog behind me to keep up.

It took me a couple of rounds to get my fight head on. The Greek lad started quickly, built an early lead. I couldn't settle. I was boxing like a schoolboy again. My mind had just not adjusted. I knew I had to calm down. I started to relax a bit, and get my range. At the end of the first round it was even. From there I was able to step it up. The cobwebs were off. My timing came back and I just put my foot down. I stopped him easily, in the third round, but not before hitting the canvas. It was only a slip. The crowd went crazy. They thought their man had knocked me down. He hadn't. He was nowhere near me. I got up and finished the job in style.

After every fight you had to do your media stuff. That was a new experience. I had never done a post-fight press conference before. When I got to the press zone there were loads of British reporters, newspapers, radio and television, cramming behind the metal barriers. Philip Pope, the Great Britain team press officer, said he had never seen anything like it. After that they had to set up a special press conference after every bout just for the British press. That had never happened before. Terry had been out at the Sydney Olympics in Audley Harrison's corner. He had never seen anything like it either. And Audley won gold in Sydney.

It was a great start, stopping the Greek boxer on home turf. My confidence surged. I went straight to the draw sheet. As expected the Bulgarian was next. The odds were stacked in his favour. He won at the first qualifiers in Croatia, where I went out in the first round. All the experts predicted a Bulgarian win. Outside of the British camp I did not have a single supporter. There is something inside me that fires in situations like that. It goes back to the early days when I first walked into the gym. I just love the action, the fight. Let me at them.

I had trained really hard for this. Making the 60 kilos limit was never an issue. I walked around bang on the weight. I was just so ready to go. There was a day's break between each fight. The day after a bout I used to go down to the running track and train. The first day I was there it was packed, boxers trying to make weight, athletes, everybody fine-tuning for competition. It was an incredible atmosphere to be around the world's best athletes in such a confined environment. I was learning by the second, eating up the experience. As the competition progressed, there would be a little more space to work in. By the time I reached the final the place was practically deserted. People did not hang around. Once their competition was over, in whatever sport, they were gone.

So I did my running, kept my mind sharp, and sketched out a mental game plan for the Bulgarian. I was confident. I was not going to let him settle, give him time to plant his feet. I wanted a fast start this time, jump on him straight away. I knew if I gave him any space he would pick me off. He had long arms, very dangerous, a good, accurate puncher. Mentally I was much better prepared for the second bout.

We had the same long walk around the arena to my corner. Just in case, Terry held on to my robe. He did not want me skipping off again. He had nothing to worry about this time. Terry judged the pace perfectly. By the time I reached the ring my head was as clear as a bell. We had gone over the fight again and again. Terry was very confident. It helped that a lot of my preparations had been done working with southpaws. Four of my five opponents at the Olympics were unorthodox. Neil Perkins was a southpaw, too. All the work I did with him paid off.

I adapted quickly, came out fast, edged in front. It was tight. I just kept to my plan. I went into the second round a point in front. The round followed a similar pattern. I was pleased. I was frustrating him. And I felt so strong. I think I must have been the fittest boxer in Athens. I was in the best shape of my life, had loads left in the tank. In the third round he started to tire. He was getting more and more frustrated. Then he started to make mistakes. I was catching him with some good shots. By the fourth I knew I was winning the fight. I just had to keep my composure. When he came in range I hit him, then moved again. That's how it went, hit and move, hit and move. Near the end his shoe lace came undone. He went into his corner to get it tied and his body slumped. You could see he was beaten. This was supposed to be a tough fight for me. I came through it pretty much unscathed. He didn't trouble me at all, and this was the European champion. At the press conference after the Greek fight, the boxing writers were saying how tough it would be. They didn't really think I had the experience or the know-how to handle the Bulgarian. After I beat him, they started talking medals.

I didn't really want to put that kind of pressure on myself. I didn't know any of the press blokes then. I know them all now. They are mostly nice fellas. Back then it was just the same faces after every fight. I had another bout before a medal could be won. But they had me winning already. I suppose it was a better story back home. The thing is not many of them knew anything about the amateur game. None of the national newspaper boys had seen me box as an amateur. They were making assumptions about fights without really knowing anything about me or the opponents.

Next up I was facing the Asian champion, a tough lad from Korea. On paper it was anything but easy. This was the Olympics, after all. And he was one of the few opponents that we did not have any video footage of. In terms of experience he was way ahead of me. They all were.

Back home things were starting to take off. In the Olympic village Terry did a brilliant job of shielding me from the attention. I wasn't really aware of the excitement I was causing. Terry decided which papers I should read, which TV programmes I should watch. He basically took control of me in the village, deciding which interviews I should do and everything like that. I was still a boy. I couldn't say no. I would have been up half the night talking to reporters if they had asked me. Terry made sure I did only what was necessary. His experience with Audley in Sydney came in very useful. I'm not sure Terry enjoyed that time as much. Audley liked to do things his way. Terry was like Mick. He was old school. He did the coaching, called the shots, the boxer did the fighting. With Audley that wasn't always the way it worked. He wanted to call the shots. That led to the odd confrontation. With me, Terry could do more or less what he wanted. He managed everything. It helped that I had slipped into Athens largely under the radar. I was the only British boxer at the Olympics. Nobody knew who I was and people weren't expecting much. In Sydney Audley told everybody that he was heading for gold. That brought added pressure because no British boxer had won a gold medal at the Olympics for more than thirty years.

At the drug test after beating the Bulgarian, I saw this other lad. It was funny. I said to Terry, look at the arms on him, they're massive. He was so stocky, legs like tree trunks, looked really strong. It turned out to be the Korean I was facing next. You can tell from a fighter's build how they are going to fight. It was clear he wouldn't be boxing me. He was a fighter. He'd be rushing straight in.

That's just what he did. From the first bell he came flying out. I was ready. I had the jab out early. Every time he came in range I caught him with the right hand over the top, the same right hand that I had injured in Korea. I didn't feel a thing. Then towards the end of the round I dropped him with a big right. I went back to the corner thinking, yeah, I have got him now. You could see it in his eyes. He was blinking like mad. He was hurt and he was given a standing eight count by the referee and the referee then said, box. I charged in, hit him with a combination, then another. The referee stopped the fight. It was the only stoppage victory of the whole tournament by any fighter. Others had won early on the points rule, but not by stoppage. Better than that I was through to the semi-finals and a guaranteed bronze medal.

I couldn't believe how easy it was. I couldn't take it in at first. Everybody else could. From that moment on, things started to get very big. I went back to the lodge in the village. I caught a clip of myself on the TV. It was the BBC flagging up my next fight.

That was a massive moment for me. Check that, man. That's me over there on the TV. I was buzzing off that. Until then Terry had worked his magic. I had no idea about the kind of reaction I was getting back home. I was treating it like any other tournament. I had no idea it would get so big. I had won the World Championships, European qualifiers. I thought it would be the same as that. As I discovered later, nothing would ever be the same as that.

I noticed the difference straight away when the other athletes started coming over to me for tickets to watch me fight. All the physios were talking about me, a lot of the staff and team members. The place was buzzing with boxing, and all the talk was about me. I would ring my mates back home in Bolton and it was just as mad there. Oh, man, you're killing it, they would say. You are all over the telly, man, on the news, everywhere.

In the village a bloke from the BBC showed me some British papers, the *Sun*, the *Mirror*, etc. They had me on the front pages. David Beckham was nowhere. That's when it hit me. That's when I realised how big a story it was. I couldn't comprehend it. I did not know what it meant. But I knew it was big news. That was really exciting for me. It was the same for Terry when he called home. His wife told him it was like the World Cup. Everybody stopped when I was fighting. The streets were empty. There was a big screen in Trafalgar Square. It seemed like the whole of London was packed in around Nelson's Column cheering me on.

About that time I remember watching in the village when Maria Sharapova beat Venus Williams in the tennis. Ian said, look at that, Amir, that could be you beating Kindelan, youth getting the better of experience. That helped to build my confidence. Why not? I thought. By then I was thinking only of winning gold. In Cyprus, Audley Harrison had come out to see me. That was a big thing for me. He had given me a few tips, a few dos and don'ts. Now I was getting close, I remembered what he had said. That helped a lot. I also had Naseem Hamed on the phone, telling me I was brilliant, that I was going to be champ. Lennox Lewis called, too. I was in the village at the time, but he spoke to Ian, wishing me well. There were text messages galore. They just did not stop coming. It was like a dream. There was just too much to take in.

It was a relief to get back to the boxing. The draw had panned out as we thought. I was fighting the Kazakh in the semis. He had done his homework. I was nervous. He started fast. I kept getting caught with stupid shots. After one shot I said to myself, come on, you need to move. I was down on points. Not much but enough to make things awkward. At the end of the first round I was two points behind. I started to think one punch at a time. Hit him, score a point. Hit him again, score another point. Right, I'm level now. I started working properly from there. The one thing I knew about him was that he tired late in fights. I got back to the corner at the end of the second thinking I was in control. In fact I was still behind. I could not believe it. I hit him with what I thought were proper scoring shots, but the judges had not marked them. The electronic scoring system is difficult to work out sometimes. When you think you have done well but haven't scored it can be heart-breaking. It was my heart that saved me. I could easily have lost that fight. I was so close to the final. I had to do something. I gritted my teeth and went for it. I kept the tempo going, kept the pace high. I kept looking for signs that he was tiring, kept throwing shots. He tried to slow it down, tried to hold on to me to stop me throwing punches. That's when the points started to flow. It was like hitting the jackpot on a slot machine. The points started to go up and up and up. At the end of the third I was ten points ahead. I was setting my feet, catching him at will. I had worked him out. The last round was a breeze. That was it, a silver medal. It was pandemonium. I was just so happy.

The post-fight period was very busy. More interviews, more

emails, texts, everybody wishing me well. Kindelan had won his semi-final against a Russian. There was just the two of us left. I had come a long way from that defeat in the first qualifier in Croatia. Kindelan didn't look too good in the semis. I could smell gold. I was convinced I would win it. It was the biggest fight at the Olympics. Kindelan was the superstar, up against a seventeen-year-old kid who had succeeded against all expectation. It was like a movie script. Everywhere I went people were coming up to me. Even Kindelan approached me. He never talks to anyone. He's always stone-faced. People were scared of him. But at the weigh-in he came up to me and said well done, gave me a big smile and hugged me. I felt really proud that he had done that. This was sport after all. People knock boxing. It's brutal this, barbaric that. It's not. It is about discipline and respect. He respected me, and I respected him.

It was nerve-racking waiting behind the curtain to be announced before the final. The MC spoke Greek for a bit, mentioned Kindelan's name then he walked out into the lights. Then it was my turn. All I could see were British flags everywhere. You wouldn't believe how good that makes you feel. I felt like I had an army behind me in that ring. The arena was packed, full of athletes. Our 100-metre relay runners were there, the rowers, loads of famous people. Olympic boxing finals are like world title fights in Las Vegas, everybody wants to be there and be seen there.

The bell went. I started well. But he was a very clever boxer. He knew every move in the book. At the end of the first round I was just ahead. That was a bit disappointing. I felt it should have been more. I was catching him and finding it relatively straightforward. Remember, six weeks before he beat me pretty easily according to the scorecards. This bout was a different matter. The second round went to Kindelan. The third round also went to Kindelan but it was close. He always seemed to be one step ahead. He countered everything I tried. He made his experience count. Every time I caught him, he would come straight back. Those rounds proved the difference. He edged in front. The last round was scored even. I had stemmed the tide but couldn't make up the lost ground. When the bell went I knew I had lost. But I still couldn't quite believe it. I have since watched the fight a dozen times, scored it myself. There is barely a point in it either way.

Afterwards in the changing room he came up to me again. He gave me a hug and said I would be a great champion one day, a gold medallist in Beijing. He was very respectful. I was the only boxer to have given him a fight. It was his second gold medal, his 360th bout at senior level to my fourteenth. When Terry watched him win at the World Championships in Belfast in 2001, he thought he was the best amateur fighter he had ever seen. Yet I had got within a hair's breadth of him. Losing hurt. I wanted that gold. I thought it was going to be mine.

I was sad because in my heart of hearts I knew that there was a very good chance that I would not contest another Games. There was a lot of thinking to be done before I made my decision, but I knew I had been in with the best and matched them. It was probably time for new challenges. When the dust settled silver tasted almost as good as gold. Even though I lost to Kindelan, there was a sense that I had achieved a great victory for myself, at just seventeen, and for amateur boxing in Britain. Even now when I speak to Terry, he says he has to pinch himself to remember that I won only silver. Usually silver medallists are forgotten. But in my case it was like I had won gold.

The medal ceremony was amazing. Standing on that podium with a medal around my neck was a huge thing for me. In the eyes of the boxing world I was just as big as Kindelan. The officials said that I deserved the best boxer of the tournament award, but they could not give it to me after losing in the final. Even outside of boxing mine was the name on everybody's lips. My star was rising fast. The proof of that was demonstrated the moment I arrived home.

I had only one day to gather my thoughts before leaving Athens. My dad was following on a day later. He asked Terry if I could stay at his house until he arrived back so that we could travel up to Bolton together. I thought now that it was all over there might be a few people waiting when we landed, a few papers, that's it.

The whole Olympic team travelled back together. I was stunned by the reception when we touched down at Gatwick. It was a weird feeling because I had never experienced that kind of hysteria before. The medallists all came off the plane together, but it was me people wanted to speak to. The likes of Matthew Pinsent and Kelly Holmes were there, too. I was getting the same kind of attention as they were. Crazy! No one really warned me what to expect. I just emerged into this massive frenzy. It was too much to take in. I was completely lost. I was signing autographs, answering questions. I did not know who I was talking to or what I was saying. I just went along with it.

It was good to get in the car with Terry. I was looking forward to a quiet night at his house before Dad flew in with the family the next day. When we got there all Terry's neighbours were out. It was like a mini street party. They were all waiting to say hello, offer their congratulations. It was nice, and a sign of things to come. Terry's wife, son and daughter were there, too. We decided to have an Indian takeaway, just the five of us. I went with Terry junior to pick up the food in his Chrysler Crossfire. Dead cool. In the restaurant there was a newspaper open on the side with my picture staring out. The owner saw me reading it. He looked at the picture then at me. He wasn't sure what was going on. That can't be Amir Khan in my restaurant, surely? I got a kick out of that.

The next day Terry and I went back to the airport to meet my dad, family and friends. BMI had arranged to fly the whole Khan clan, about fifteen of us, back up to Manchester for free. That had never happened to us before. When we arrived at

Manchester airport the scenes dwarfed those at Gatwick. I have never seen an airport as full in my life. I thought half of Bolton was there, people I had never seen before, people of all ages, colour and race, all crammed into every bit of space. You could not walk anywhere. The police had to work overtime to get me through the crowds.

Outside there was a big limo waiting to take me back to Bolton, a Hummer. A local firm in Bolton phoned my uncle and asked if they could send a car for me. Again everything was free. Apart from winning a medal I was pretty certain I was the same person that had left a few weeks before. I hadn't changed. What had was the way people behaved towards me. I've since discovered that as a famous person you rarely have to pay for anything.

By the time we got to Bolton it was almost midnight. I was shattered. All I wanted was to go inside the house and have a cup of tea. Talk about misread a situation. We couldn't get near the street, never mind the house. The place was rammed with people as far as you could see. It was absolutely mad. Every one of them had come to see me. They had been waiting like that for ages. I finally stepped out and people started hugging me, shaking my hand. Two weeks before I was a nobody. Now this. There is nothing in school that prepares you for the kind of thing that was happening to me. You just learn as you go along.

The next morning it started again. There was a knock at the door. My dad answered. It was the press. They wanted pictures. Pictures? What do you want pictures for? When they explained to my dad that it would be easier for everybody if I made an appearance I wandered out with a cup of tea, smiled and got it over with. Except that it is never really over with.

Two days later my uncle threw a welcome home party for me. Great, at least it will be a small, family do, a chance to see all my friends and family again. Not quite. The TV and papers were there again. We were on first-name terms now. They were not the only gatecrashers. There was a knock at the door. As usual my dad did the honours. There were five people stood on the step, all Irish. They had travelled over that day, arrived in the centre of Bolton and jumped in a taxi asking to be taken to Amir Khan's house. The driver knew us, knew about the party and brought them straight around to my uncle's. I posed for some pictures with them, signed a few autographs, then that was it. They went on their way. How mad is that? The next day there was another party, then another. It went on like that for a couple of months, dinners, receptions, etc.

Two weeks before I was just another anonymous seventeen-year-old. Now I was the most famous teenager in Britain, riding around Bolton in an open-top bus. Only footballers get to do that. I even met the Queen. I asked her if she watched the fights. When you are introduced to the Queen you are not supposed to ask her questions or start conversations. You wait for her to speak to you. I knew about making a bow. They had told us about that. I didn't know about the rest. Buckingham Palace had never been on our radar in Bolton. I was nervous. All the athletes were. You don't know what to say, do you? It was mind-blowing. I'm just a normal lad from a town in the north-west of England. I never thought I'd be stood in the Queen's front room. Her bodyguard was there. I reckon he must have been scared of me. The Queen was great. Oh, she said, you're the boxer. She told me that she had seen my fights, that I had done such a lot for the country.

At another reception, to promote Britain's Olympic bid, the Prime Minister Tony Blair asked me for my autograph for his kids. He's a fan. So is Tessa Jowell. She asked me to be an ambassador for boxing in schools. How could I say no after the way boxing had sorted my life out?

3

Wallflower to Poster Boy

There is a massive poster on the wall in the reception at Smithills School. I'm on it. I share top billing with the other famous pupils that went to the school: my cousin Saj Mahmood, Ronnie Irani, another cricketer, comedian Dave Spikey and Paul Nicholls, who was probably the most famous lad in Bolton when he was in *EastEnders* a few years ago. Paul's real name is Greenhalgh. He was the Brad Pitt of Smithills. He could act, too, and spoke brilliantly. The teachers always gave him a starring role on the school stage. That made him popular with the girls, and just about the opposite with the lads. He used to get loads of stick off them. When I was there the school was better known for its music. It has performance arts status. Smithills were the National Youth Brass Band Champions in 2004 and 2005 and went on to win the world title in America. A massive achievement.

I had just begun boxing competitively when I started there. The Asian lads at the school weren't really into sport. They were too busy being hard guys. I never used to get involved in all that. I was too into my boxing. I was a good student. Boxing taught me discipline. I could just hear Mick drumming it into me about doing things the proper way. I bought into that. My tearaway days were over. I came into my own more when I started boxing for junior titles and fighting in international tournaments. Before that the teachers and the other kids didn't really know much about me. I was quiet. Kept myself to myself. Stayed out of trouble.

In my early days at Smithills I was picked up as a runner. I ran like the wind. I've always done it as part of my boxing training. Mr Dickinson, my PE teacher, spotted it straight away. He thought I was just a talented athlete. He was surprised when I told him I was into boxing. I remember he put his hands up like the pads and said, go on then, let's see you. I didn't mean to hurt him. Bang, bang, quick as a flash. He turned away wringing his hands. They were the only punches I ever threw in school. Like all comprehensive schools in big towns, Smithills had its problems. The troublemakers were called 'challenging pupils'. There was the odd flare-up between the Asian lads and the white kids. No one bothered me.

My mates at Bolton Community College where I went later would not have recognised me at Smithills. At college I was the man. Here I was always in the background, quietly getting on with things. Because I had a good attitude I never had a problem with the teachers. Mr Dickinson was great. When things started to take off for me as a junior amateur the school would always support me. Once Mr Dickinson got a local Asian businessman to sponsor me. Smithills has one of the best sports halls in the North-west. Mr Dickinson's daughter had twelve international caps in basketball and she said she never played in a venue as good as that. Mr Dickinson wanted to use it as a boxing venue, put a ring in the middle, seats around the outside and a bar for the spectators upstairs. That would be mad. One day, maybe. There is also a private health club in the school. The gym is brilliant, running machines, bikes, rowing machines, a proper fitness club. Towards the end of my time there when I was competing internationally I used to go in at lunch times and pound away on the treadmill. It felt great. Nothing like Bury ABC. Everything was brand new.

It helped that my cousin Saj had been through the school

before me. He obviously stood out as a cricketer. Like me he was a role model for the Muslim community through sport. He could do everything. Before him it was Ronnie Irani. Ronnie has a Pakistani background through his dad's side of the family. I don't know him but he was a legend at Smithills. When Ronnie turned up for school cricket matches his bag was bigger than the school kit bag. Full of Gray Nicholls stuff. He used to cost the school money. He was forever whacking the balls out of the school grounds. They could never find them. Once he lost five balls in one over. Mr Dickinson reckons it cost the school £70. And that was twenty years ago. He could bowl a bit, too. He would have the ball whizzing past the batsman's ears. In one match Mr Dickinson was umpiring Ronnie's first ball went fizzing through at chin height. Mr Dickinson pulled him up. Ronnie, come off three paces for your next ball. That was three paces, said Ronnie. After four deliveries Mr Dickinson had to take Ronnie out of the attack. He was too quick. Quicker than Saj at the same age. Ronnie could do anything; he played basketball for the North of England. He went for England trials. He was a big personality even then. Mr Dickinson's favourite cricketer at Smithills. Sorry, Saj.

When I began to win things the school switched on, started to understand a bit more about what I was doing. Because Saj played cricket, the school had him down as a sporting superstar from the off. Boxing wasn't part of the school sports curriculum. It was only when I started appearing in the *Bolton Evening News* that people began to take notice of me at school. There were write-ups about me in the school bulletin. I had to get up on stage after winning titles. I hated that. I couldn't box for the school. But I could run.

The road outside the school, Smithills Deane Road, takes you straight up to the moors. I used to run up that road in training. Killer it was. We looked for a house up there after I turned pro but my mum didn't like it. She said it was too remote. She likes to have people around her. The only living things she would have had for company up there were sheep. There are a few old farmhouses scattered about. But no neighbours. The views are brilliant. On clear, sunny days you can see for miles, all the way across Bolton and down into Manchester. After running up there, competing for the school was no problem. No one could keep up with me at Smithills. I always won the inter-form competitions. I won Greater Manchester titles at cross country and 1,500 metres. I was picked for national trials but couldn't make it because it clashed with boxing. Mr Dickinson reckons I could have made it as an athlete. But boxing always came first.

A year after leaving Smithills I was an Olympic silver medallist. Unbelievable. I didn't forget my old teachers. When they had a big reception for me at Bolton Town Hall I made sure that Mr Dickinson and a few of the others were there. I'm back outside the school gates quite a bit. My brother Haroon is still there. When my dad can't pick him up I go and get him in the Beamer. When I left I never thought I'd be back two years later picking up my brother in a convertible BMW.

After Smithills I moved on quickly in every way. As soon as I qualified for the Olympics it went mad in Bolton. There was no escape from the local media. The fact that I was still in education, in the first year of my course at Bolton Community College, made it an even better story. Every time my mates turned on the TV there was a shot of me at a desk and my tutor Graham Roberts giving an interview. If you ask Graham about it now he uses technical terms like 'piece to camera' when he tells the story. He was like a pro broadcaster. That shows how much exposure I was getting. It was all new to me and great for Bolton College.

On the day I made it through to the Olympic final, Graham received a call from reception saying that Sky TV were outside and would like to talk to him. When he went to meet them it was like a film set. There was a complete outside broadcast unit waiting to greet him. It was on the same day that Paula Radcliffe stopped running in the 10,000 metres. That was a massive story after she did the same in the marathon.

Sky had sent a reporter to her athletics club and had come to Graham straight after speaking to her former coach. They gave him a five-minute warning and told him to put his earpiece in. He was a slick operator by this time. As soon as the students twigged what was happening there was a mad scrum around the van. All they could see was Graham talking to a camera with his earpiece in. The questions came from the presenter in the Sky studio in London. I'm surprised they did not offer Graham a job. Maybe they did. He would never have taken it, unless they moved the studios to Bolton. Graham is like me, he loves Bolton too much to ever leave it. He grew up in Bury, where I trained with Mick, and started working in IT before retraining as a teacher. He did his degree at Bolton, his teaching qualifications at Bolton and his master's degree at Bolton.

TV were not the only people wanting to hear from my teacher. The local radio stations were all over him as well. GMR wanted Graham on their morning slot. That was a smaller production. The radio guy turned up at Graham's house at 7 a.m. and interviewed him in his front room before he went to work. He had already spoken to an Asian radio station by then in a telephone interview. Again from home. By then he was fluent in Amir Khan stories. It was like reading from a script.

They say your school days are the best. I didn't really understand what people were on about until I walked through the doors of Bolton Community College. I wouldn't change anything about my life now. I just wish that my student days could have lasted a bit longer. I would love to have gone to university with my mates. I was doing a BTech national diploma in sports development and fitness, which is the equivalent of A levels. It is a two-year course that would have given me the qualification I needed to go to uni. About 60 per cent of the students on the course went on to higher education. That was my plan. I was still at Smithills when I decided that the course at BCC was the best for me. At that time I was still thinking about the Beijing Games in 2008. That would have been perfect timing. I would have finished my degree just before going to China for the Games. Even though I had shifted my thinking after Louisiana, Athens was still a long way off. When I started at the college in September 2003 I thought that was where I would be for the next two years.

The course was brilliant. It suited me perfectly because it was based around practical work. All the assessments were set around practical tests. There was some desk work involved but not as much as traditional A-level courses. If I had gone to North College, where most of my top mates went to do their A levels, I know I would definitely have messed about. It's a good school. My cousin Rakeb goes there. It's in the grounds of Smithills School. But I needed a change.

Most of the students on the course were sports mad. Football was the big thing. The lads were all good players. Miles better than me. But they realised by then that they were not going to make it as a pro. For lads in that position the course was perfect. I was the only kid there from a boxing background. Nobody knew anything about my amateur career. They did not have a clue that I had a bucketful of medals at home and that I was trying to get to Athens to represent Britain at the Olympics. That is one of the reasons I enjoyed it so much. I could get away from the intensity of competition. It was like a break for me, a place I did not have to talk about boxing. Don't get me wrong. I loved my sport. But here I loved just being Amir, one of the lads. And I was one of the lads. There were just three Asians in a group of thirty-two, me, Saj and Ash. As the year went on we had that class boxed off. We were the cool guys at the back that everybody wanted to chill with. If they gave out degrees for chilling I'd have been on for a double first. King chiller. That was me.

I started out pretty quiet. That's what I'm like. To the tutors I was this nice Asian lad at first. I didn't give any chat to anybody. I just got on with my work. I think they thought I was an athlete or something. I was built like a classic 1,500-metre runner. I didn't look like a boxer, and because I didn't talk about it they never guessed. The first inkling anybody had was during the two-week induction period. Graham did this ice-breaking exercise where people were paired off and had to interview each other. After that you had to stand up in front of the group and talk about yourself. It was like a confidence builder. I found it nerve-racking. I was one of the youngest in my class, a bit shy. I was teamed up with a lad called Ian. He was much older than me, a mature student about twenty-six. There were lots of obvious questions like what school did you go to? What's your favourite food? It ended with the question, what is your career ambition? I said that I was going to win an Olympic medal. Ian laughed it off, didn't give it a second thought. This was Bolton Community College, full of kids who wanted to be joiners, plumbers or hairdressers. I was yet to turn seventeen. Olympics my foot. Ian smiles about that now. I remember before that drawing the Olympic rings on the front of my folder and telling Saj to remember the date because I was going to win a medal one day.

The boxing thing stayed under the radar pretty well until I had to ask for time off to go to training camps. I didn't really like to talk about it much. I didn't want people to think I was chatting down to them, I'm a boxer, I'm tough, I'm famous, I've done this, done that. I just wanted to be treated like a normal lad. People started to take it more seriously when I began to go off to tournaments and qualifiers. They knew about it but did not really understand the level I was at. I set off at college in the right way, always keeping up with my work. When I had to take time off I went through the proper channels, requesting permission in writing and phoning in to make sure Graham knew where I was. He used to stick post-it notes all over his desk so he could keep up with my whereabouts. During the second term when the ABA finally decided I could try for the Olympics it started to get a bit mad. I was off to training camps and then the qualifiers started. Inevitably things went a bit astray.

One morning my phone rang. It was Graham. Amir, where are you? Why are you not in college this morning? I was sat in an airport in Bulgaria waiting for my bags to come off the luggage belt. Graham had forgotten. His post-it note must have fallen down the back of his computer. It was the tournament that sparked the madness, where I finally qualified for the Games. The students were well tuned in to what I was doing by then. They followed that particular tournament on the internet. There was no coverage through conventional media channels so they logged on to a Bulgarian website. No one could understand a word. They just picked out my name and the British flag on the bout sheet and worked out what was happening when the flag appeared in the next round.

When I got back Bolton College was a different place. It was the start of a process that I have still not fully come to terms with. I went from being Amir to being Amir Khan, public property, overnight. People I didn't really know would spot me and say, that's Amir Khan. It was weird hearing my name spoken like that. I had only ever been Amir before. Now I was Amir Khan, boxer. In a sense I preferred it when I was just Amir. I liked having something back in reserve.

The lads at college might not have taken me seriously at first when Ian told them what I had said to him, but they knew I must have been good at something when we did the first few assignments. The course was split into eighteen different units. You had to pass them all to get the qualification. Fitness testing was one of the first units we did. We had to learn about the different tests that you do to monitor fitness. One of them was the bleep test. Everybody in the class had to do it. Basically you ran backwards and forwards in between the bleeps. The bleeps got faster and faster but you still had to cover the distance. People were really going for it. No one wanted to be the first to give up. If you got to level ten you were going some. If you reached twelve you were at an excellent level of fitness. One by one people started to drop. It came down to me and Saj. All the other students watched in amazement as we ran up and down the sports hall. Eventually Saj dropped out. I crashed through the level sixteen barrier and stopped. Graham had never seen anyone hit that level in five years. It is still a record as far as he is aware and I wasn't properly fit at the time. That earned me the respect of the group and set me up for the other units.

It was hard going at times. Some lads turned up on the course expecting to play football for two years. They got a big kick in the backside. You had to take it seriously or you had no chance of getting through. I got my head down and did the work. The reflective practitioner unit was about monitoring performance in your own sport, setting yourself goals and targets. That was the first written assignment. Mine was all about boxing. There was a unit on coaching where you learned about the theory of coaching, building up to delivering your own session. Mine was on boxing. There was a psychology course, where you looked at stress and anxiety in sport. That made me laugh. Sometimes you can think too much about things. I was more of a doer. At training camp the boxing coaches would ask you to lie down and do breathing exercises and imagery, where you see yourself in winning situations, stuff like that. I used to lie there bored, staring into space.

I got more out of the anatomy course, where you learn about the muscles you use for particular sports. I looked at that from my point of view as a boxer. It was great learning about the effects of weight loss, hydrating the muscles, the specific muscles used most by fighters. I learned loads of technical stuff about fitness and boxing that I never knew before. That kept me interested. 'Sport in society', and 'ethics and values' in sport were the tricky bits, big projects set by the exam board. That part of the course looked at stuff like race, gender, disability, things I didn't really think about much. I got stuck into it, though. It got me thinking about why Asian lads don't get involved in football much. Why they stick to particular sports and not others. There are not enough Asians involved in boxing. It was good to try to get to the bottom of things like that. It comes down to culture in the end. As far as football is concerned, there aren't enough Asian lads playing in local club teams. A team has just started up in Bolton exclusively for Asian kids. I'm not sure that is the right way to go. Only eleven players can play at once for a start. Even if you have five age groups, that's not enough to make a difference. If I had that attitude in boxing I would never have got in the ring. Most of the lads I trained with were white. It never bothered me.

I turned up one morning after being away for a week at the first Olympic qualifier. It hadn't gone well. Graham said, Amir, you do know you've got your coaching session this morning? No problem, I said. Had you remembered? No, I said, but I'll do it anyway. Have you done your session plan? I don't need one. Amir, it's an observed session, it contributes to your overall marks, you need a session plan to show that you are working to a set of aims and objectives. We agreed that I would take the session and write the plan out afterwards. It was the first time Graham had really seen me in action. He was impressed.

I just did it off the top of my head. I got the students in a big circle. I stayed in the middle. I took them through a basic warm-up, the kind of stuff I did every time I went to a boxing gym, then I got them going on a few basic techniques: shadow boxing, footwork, balance, punches, combinations, throwing a jab, a right hand. Before I knew it an hour had gone. It was only supposed to last forty-five minutes. They absolutely loved it. They knew where I had just been. They were aware then what level I was performing at, that I was a serious athlete. Apart from that, it was different stuff for them. They had never done any boxing training in their lives. They were used to doing things like football, indoor hockey, volleyball and basketball. No one had ever taken a boxing session before. I was able to show that I could put a safe and effective session together for boys and girls. The girls loved it as much as the lads. Some of the sessions were recorded on video. Mine wasn't. I think Graham regrets that now. Maybe I'll go back one day to do a special session for him when I'm a world champion.

At the start of the second and third terms we had to complete assessment forms, a kind of report where we awarded ourselves marks in the different disciplines and wrote down comments. It's about identifying strengths and weaknesses, areas where you need to improve. The award marks ran from one to five. One was excellent, five rubbish. I didn't give myself a one in anything. I didn't score a five either. Attendance was my downfall, for obvious reasons. I gave myself a three for that.

This is what I wrote on my first report in January 2004, eight months before I fought for Olympic gold against Mario Kindelan.

I could improve my attendance. I would ring in college when I'm absent. I have no problems working with others. And I enjoy all the subjects.

For my three-point action plan I wrote:

Put more hours into this subject outside of college. Ring in when sick or absent. Hand in course work before deadlines.

This is what Graham wrote:

A capable student who works well in the group and appears to enjoy the course. He needs to focus on applying himself to his studies while managing his time well.

Within three months of writing that first report I had qualified for the Games. When I look back now sitting down to write it seems a million years away. That's how rapidly my life has changed.

We wrote our second reports in April. By then I had missed loads of time to go to qualifiers and other events. It was mad. I loved college, but outside of it things were changing fast. This is what I said in my second report:

> Attendance dropped because of boxing training. My punctuality has been the same. I work well within the group. My performance in written work has dropped because I don't like written work.

And my three-point action plan:

> Continue to perform and maintain a good balance between training and studying. Need to manage time well over the next term. Make sure I don't fall too far behind on work. Develop research skills using internet and books.

I meant what I wrote. I had a great laugh but I took the course seriously. Boxing helped me in class. I was very disciplined. And if I fell behind I felt bad about it, like missing a training session. If I commit to something I do it. Though I had qualified for the Olympics, in my mind I was coming back to college in September for another year. I was going for gold but had no idea what winning a medal might mean at that stage. So I kept up with the work right until the end of term. I didn't get any special treatment. Graham would say to me, look, Amir, you've got assignments. I know you're busy. I'll help you out as much as I can but come on, man, get on with it.

That first year at college was a special period in my life. Everything seemed to be changing at once. The boxing was taking off massively and so was my personal life. I felt like a student instead of a schoolboy. That was massive for me. I had a great time at Smithills, too, but it was a completely different experience. At Bolton College there were students of all ages from all sorts of backgrounds. At Smithills it was about a 50/50 split, Asian and white. At the college it was nowhere near that.

We referred to teachers by their first names, not sir. They spoke to us as equals, as adults. There were no detentions or stuff like that. You either got on with your work or you got out. We could wear what we wanted. I couldn't believe it at first. It was all about getting students to take responsibility for themselves. In boxing I had been doing that for a long time. I couldn't cut any corners in my sport without hurting myself.

It was cool to be calling my teacher Graham. For me it made me work. I wanted to do the stuff because I didn't want to let Graham and the other tutors down. Graham was brilliant. He was more like a mate. You could talk to him about anything. I used to go down to his office, have a laugh with him. He'd rip us, we'd rip him. Once when Saj and Ash had been messing about, Graham put wanted posters all over the college, pictures of Saj and Ash: If you see these two on the premises report them to the principal at once, something like that. I didn't fancy that treatment myself. Graham had the power to do embarrassing stuff like that so I always stayed in his good books.

The college building was the opposite of what I had known at school. Smithills was in a really nice part of Bolton, heading out of the town towards the moors. It gets its name from the country hall and park next door. The park stands in 2,000 acres. You can see all over Bolton from up there. People are surprised when they see it. Not scruffy at all. Bolton College was bang in the middle of town on Manchester Road. I think the building belonged to the RAF many years ago, an old technical college used by the air force. The teachers say it is bomb-proof. It wasn't lad-proof. Sorry, Graham. It felt cool to be in there because it didn't feel like a school. It looked more like a factory. It was massive. There were more than 10,000 students taking vocational courses. The college is looking for another, more modern site in the town centre. I loved it. The basement was a huge space with loads of rooms off long corridors. Smithills had big windows and was very light. Down in that basement it was dark. That is where the workshops are based. Most of the lads at the college were starting out in some sort of construction trade, joinery, plumbing, bricklaying. It was like a building site down there most days. They would have to build things like house extensions from scratch then knock them down again to let the next group use all the materials.

We spent most of our time in the sports hall and other multi-purpose spaces doing practical assessments. When we weren't in there we were in the refectory, me and Saj chilling, looking cool, trying to impress the girls off the hair and beauty course. They used to walk around college all day carrying dummies' heads with wigs on. At first we were really quiet. By the end of the year I think we knew the names of every girl in the college. I could never have done that at Smithills. It was all innocent stuff, a bit of fun in the lunch break. We used to walk into the canteen and everybody would go, Amir, Amir, come and sit with me. Then they would say, Amir, I'm practising massage this afternoon, why don't you come up? Or why don't you let me cut your hair? There were some nice-looking girls, too. I never did go for a massage.

I was finding my feet in a different world, spreading my wings. Me and Saj, we had it boxed off. In a way we were the roots of the class. If we weren't in there, the class wasn't running. We even had the car park guy locked down. Parking is a nightmare at the college. You have to get there at the crack of dawn to get a space. At first the guy would say it's only for teachers. By the time we left he was saving a space for us. We just used to talk to him, chill with him, work him around to our way of thinking. It was handy at lunch times. You could go back to the car and chill with your mates. Sometimes we 'ate out'. For a laugh we'd take a couple of mates, white lads, over to Daubhill to get an Asian takeaway. We'd get a curry and watch their eyes water in the back. That hot enough for you, lads? They loved chilling with us. That was mad. You never used to see Asian lads chilling with white guys. We did it all the time. I've mixed with different cultures all my life. It was a natural thing for me.

Everyone wanted to be our friends. It was tops. People look at me now and think I have got everything. They don't realise that I had everything before the Olympics only without the money. I enjoyed life at college as much as I am enjoying it now. I had girls asking me out then just like they do now. I'm one of those guys who has always got on with people. I have a laugh. If I could I would love to go to university as well. I know I would have the same laugh there. My mate goes to uni in Preston. I go up there to see him. I'm almost part of the class when I go there. We have a proper laugh.

Bolton College encouraged the students to mix and socialise. I would have given myself a one for that in my report. Qualifying for the Olympics didn't hurt in that department. It was like big respect from everybody. Even the bricklayers. Massive lads they were. Some of them really tough. I never had any problem with them. If there ever was any trouble I would have fifty brickies behind me. I got on great with everybody. No one ever called me Paki.

When the cameras started coming in to film me at college, my mates loved it more than I did. They would sit in the background pretending to be writing then run home and put the telly on to see if they were on the local news. Some were even interviewed themselves. What's he like then? What is it like being in the same class as an Olympic boxer? They all had to say nice things. That killed me. In another sense all the attention started to cramp my style a bit. I was embarrassed by it at times.

When I came back with silver it was madder than ever. Great publicity for the college, though. There was a big poster of me at the reception. The college put on this big welcome-back press conference. The college principal and Graham were on the top table with me. My dad and uncle were also sitting up there. There was an open microphone. Anybody could ask questions. It was embarrassing for me to be coming into college with my dad. When I left for the Olympics I was the top chiller, king of cool, too cool to be seen in college with my dad, that's for sure.

Later before term started I came back to college on my own without telling anybody. I wandered around to the staff room and knocked on the door. Graham was inside. We had a chat about the Olympics. I told him a few stories, like the one about the knock on the changing-room door before the final. I told my dad I didn't want to speak to any more people. I had loads of people wishing me well, but the clock was ticking now. Kindelan was just around the corner. I needed to focus. The person knocked again, said he just wanted a quick word. The door opened and in walked Sylvester Stallone. He sounded just like Rocky Balboa. I was a massive underdog. I think he liked that. He wished me luck and went on his way. Graham laughed. Sylvester has never made it to Bolton.

Graham asked if he could see the medal sometime. I said sure and pulled it out of my pocket. He couldn't believe that I was wandering around college with my Olympic medal stuffed in my pocket. It was the safest place. At least that way my nieces and nephews couldn't get their hands on it. They had been running around the house with it around their necks pretending to be Olympic champions. The medal got passed around the staff room. The teachers took turns to slip it around their necks. They were just like kids.

When we came in September, everything was different for me. For the rest of the lads it was just the same. Saj started where he left off, chasing me round college with a fire extinguisher. I came back from the Olympics and said to the boys, look, lads, everything is different now. Everybody knows who I am. You might be chasing me with a fire extinguisher and ITV will get it on film. I can't have that. It's bad media for us. Yeah, yeah, they said. No problem. So on that first day Saj was waiting for me round the corner holding a fire extinguisher. I was walking in with Ash. We spotted him. He was about 50 metres away. He had this big smile on his face. When he saw me he came charging out screaming at the top of his voice. He didn't realise that he was standing next to the staff room. Teachers and security staff came running out thinking there was a maniac on the loose. Saj copped it big time for that. Saj was a madman. He just wanted to doss about the whole time. He got an A in graphics at school. At the college there were only three or four students in his group. One was about thirty, another twenty-five. Much older than him. I knew when he switched to my sports class that he just wanted to muck about. He was always getting warnings from Graham, always on the verge of being chucked out.

I knew I would not be able to carry on as before. There was just too much happening. Graham understood. The idea of going to college was to prepare for the next stage in my life. That next stage was now. An opportunity was knocking that I had to take. I was only managing one day a week at college. I was being invited here, there and everywhere, training for the ABAs, meeting the Queen, all sorts of stuff. In November 2004 I went into college with my dad and explained to Graham that I was coming off the course. I made the decision myself. Technically I could go back any time before 2008 to finish the units. It's a nice idea. For now I'm done with college.

4

All Roads Lead to Rawalpindi

I was six or seven when I made my first trip to Pakistan. My family came from a farming village called Matore near Rawalpindi in the north of the country. Everybody knows everybody there. People were aware that I was related to Lall Khan who took his family to England. Matore is pretty much the same now as it was when my grandad left for England in 1963. It was strange yet familiar. It looked nothing like Bolton. Yet I was surrounded by family, people that I had heard my dad and uncles talking about. There were no rows of terraced houses, animals were kept around and about the houses, blue skies every day, and it was hot. When my dad was born, there was no water in the house. You had to get it from a well, or from a stand pipe in the street. There is water now but it is still very different. Time kind of stands still. When I'm there I don't even know what time it is, never mind what day it is. When it starts to get dark, I know it's night time. That's about it. There are no newspapers, nobody really watches TV in the same way. You could be on the moon for all you knew about what was going on back home. But I like it. You just chill, and drink tea, 24/7.

The house that my grandad built is still there. My aunt lives in it now. It was one of the first of its kind. Grandad was a bit of a pioneer. He broke the mould. My dad says there is a lot of him in me. The family owned land in and around Matore. My grandad was in the military. When he left the forces he decided to come to England. It was a brave move. He had a good position in Pakistan. When he arrived in England his first job was planting potatoes in Bradford, something he would never have done back home. He could not speak a word of English. It must have been tough. Harder than anything I have had to do. Compared to that, boxing is a piece of cake. Not only was the language strange, the food, culture, climate, everything was completely different. Knowing how different Pakistan felt to me on my first visit, I can't imagine how he must have felt coming to England, stepping off a plane into a strange, cold country, full of mod cons. I had my dad holding my hand when I went to Pakistan for the first time, and loads of family waiting to greet me. He had no one. It took courage to do what he did.

I remember being very excited about getting on the plane to Islamabad on my first trip out there. I didn't really think too much about where I was going. I was just so chuffed to be flying. We were going over for my uncle's wedding so there were quite a few of us. I was charging around as usual causing havoc with my cousins. When we got there the first thing I noticed was the number of people at the airport. It was mobbed, chaotic. For every person getting off the plane there must have been ten to meet them. People were so happy to see their relatives. It was a big thing. When you think that a lot of people in Matore and the other villages in that part of Pakistan still get around on foot, going to an airport must be a massive thing.

The journey from Islamabad to Matore is mad. It only takes about one hour. There are lots of stalls at the roadside, people selling things, loads of funny buses with tiny windows and decorated in amazing colours. You never see empty buses in Pakistan. There are fifty people squashed inside and another fifty hanging off the roof and the sides. They just go for it. There is no way they would allow people to pack on to buses like that in England. It would never get past the health and safety. And the cars. My dad had a scrapyard. He had better cars in his yard than they had in Pakistan. Crazy.

The other thing that I found strange was the animals – cows, goats, birds all over the place. It was a farming community. People lived off their animals in a way people hadn't in England for hundreds of years. I would see a goat and try to stroke it. The other kids thought I was crazy. They see goats every day. They just walk past them and get on with the game of cricket. Cricket is like football in England only twice as mad. If you are good at cricket in Pakistan you are the king of the playground. They play on every bit of spare ground, proper games, bowlers, batsmen, everything. Young lads charging in off long runs with their shalwar kameez blowing behind them.

I was always trying to play with the animals. One of my uncles showed me how to milk a cow. I had never seen a cow close up before. Look, he said, fresh milk. Have a drink. Being a kid I did as I was told and got warm milk all over my face. My dad still laughs about it now, me pulling on the teat spraying milk everywhere. Because life is arranged around animals and the farm, the day starts early. People are moving around by six. By the time I used to get up around 11 a.m., it seemed to me that the day's work was done. It was back to chilling and tea. They drink more tea in Pakistan than we do. Proper tea, too. It wasn't really like that of course. The atmosphere was just so much more relaxed.

My relatives were over the moon when they saw me for the first time. My grandad on my mum's side did not have any sons. He used to spoil me rotten, take me for walks, give me things. Over the years we would go back during school holidays for about three or four weeks each time. As I got older I realised how little people in Pakistan had compared to us. Material stuff. It did not bother them. They lived a stress-free life, looking after animals and taking things easy. They didn't need much money for that. We felt like millionaires in Pakistan. The shopkeepers used to have a big smile on their faces when we turned up. They used to get extra sweets and bottles of Coke in when they knew we were coming over.

Shopping was a whole new experience, full stop. In England you go into a shop and pay the price on the ticket. In Pakistan the marked price means nothing. At first I didn't know that. My cousins would say, what are you doing paying that for that stuff? Er, buying it, I would say. No, no, don't do that. As soon as I opened my mouth the shopkeeper knew I was foreign. He would see easy money coming his way. I soon got the hang of it. My dad says he feels a bit ashamed about haggling with me. I love it. They ask 2,000 rupees for something, I offer them 500. When they say no, I walk away. OK, OK, they say. You are my first sale of the day. Take it. Thanks very much. It's the same for everything except food. Mad.

People used to look at us and think we had it easy. That everybody in Europe lived the high life. They don't see how hard it is, how stressful it is for people to survive in the rat race, the daily slog from nine to five. And because the pound goes a long way over there, they think it is the same in England. They think we have got it cushy and can buy anything we want. It's a trade-off, lifestyle for wealth. You can live a long life in Matore. There are a lot of old people wandering around in their eighties and nineties. The air is fresh, there is lots of space, beautiful country-side, mountains. The life can be hard, but it passes at such a slow pace. In England you have more money in comparison to Pakistan, but you have to flog yourself to get it. And the merry-go-round never seems to stop. People are always striving to get to the next stage in their lives, for the next big thing, car, house. In Matore, nobody strives. They simply exist as they always have done. They don't understand how we live. They just see the spending power of foreigners.

Wherever we went my dad would hire a car. You would get a driver thrown in for the day all for less than a fiver, chauffeuring you everywhere. We weren't doing it to be flash. You couldn't drive over there. They don't know what a white line is. If the driver sees a gap in the traffic he fills it. As far as I can work out there aren't any rules. I don't even think you have to pass your test. I've got relatives, thirteen or fourteen years old, who have been driving since they were ten. I didn't know how to start a car at ten. Their reactions are good, I'll give them that. The most important thing is that you have a car with a horn that works. If not, you are in real trouble.

I often wonder how things would have turned out for me if my grandad had not come to Bolton. My dad says he would have gone into the army, or politics. I suppose I would have done the same. I would not be writing a book about my life as an Olympic silver medallist, that's for sure. Even though I look Pakistani, and my ancestors are all Pakistani, the locals could tell I was not from Pakistan. It didn't matter that I was fluent in the language. Just by the way you stand, walk, your manner-isms, they can tell you are foreign, from England. It's amazing. Though my uncles always filled me in on the family history, I was always viewed as a foreigner. In a nice way, though. In the village, around my own people, I felt pretty much like one of the family. In the town, in Rawalpindi, I felt more like a kid from Bolton. That is how they saw me. As I grew up and started to learn more about where I came from, it was amazing to think I could be walking past people in the street who were related to me.

As well as my grandad's house in Matore, we have a house in Rawalpindi. My dad bought it about six years ago. I think he is planning his retirement there. He can see himself going back and living like a king, being looked after by servants. It's not for me now. I love it when I'm there and when I'm older I may well go and live in Pakistan full time. At the moment I love it too much in Bolton. My dad was born in Matore, his father and mother are buried there. He sees himself as Pakistani. I can understand why he would want to go back at the end of his life, and I feel the same too. I'm Pakistani in terms of my background, but culturally I'm British, Bolton through and through.

Grandad came here to make a better life. He had nothing. He was a grafter. He was proud of never owing anybody anything. He bought his own house, one of the first to do so in the area. People used to stay with him and pay rent. That's how he saved up money to bring his family over. Grandad was a real hero to us growing up. He died before I was born but Grandma used to keep his memory alive, telling us stories about how he made the journey and settled in Bolton. Without him I wouldn't be here, doing what I do. In that sense I owe everything to him, we all do.

After planting potatoes in Bradford, he moved to Bolton where he got a job in a cotton mill. There is a photograph of him at the house in Matore stood in the mill in front of rows and rows of cotton. It was taken about 1970. You could tell how proud he was to be in that picture, wearing a suit and tie. It was kind of proof that he had made a success of the move. It is one of my favourite photos. Thirty years on my picture started appearing in the papers in Bolton. My dad says that Grandad would have been proud of that.

After a while working in the mill, he got a job at Wolstenholme's powder company. My dad remembers him coming home coated in bronze powder. It was very hard for him. But he was proud to be doing the best for his family. His family meant everything to him. When my uncle Terry finished his apprenticeship at British Aerospace, Grandad bought him a car, a Ford Cortina. He didn't even drive himself. My uncle used to drop him off at work. His mates used to say, Lall, have you won the pools? He wasn't doing it to show off. He wanted to reward his son for doing well. My dad always says if you are going to buy something, buy something good. It will hurt you to spend the money, but if you buy something cheap you will be crying every day. He got that saying from Grandad. It would have been great for him to see me now, to see how we have taken the Khan story on.

When he retired Grandad went home to build another house, this time in Rawalpindi. It is still there now, with a nice bit of land down the side of it. He phoned home to Bolton to say the house was finished and he would be back in England within a week. He never made it. A few days after finishing the house he died of a heart attack. At least he passed away in the country of his birth. When I go back to Pakistan now, to Matore, I'm known more as the grandson of Lall, rather than Amir Khan, Olympic silver medallist. He is still the reference point for the Khan family.

Things have changed a lot for those Pakistani families that arrived in Bolton in the Sixties. Back then they made Bolton like a little corner of Pakistan. They stuck with traditional ways of dressing, they cooked the same food as they ate at home and kept the same customs. Over time things have become much more Westernised in Asian families. The dress has changed completely for the younger people, who only ever wear the shalwar kameez on special occasions. My mum still wears Pakistani dress but my dad is always in his jeans and T-shirt like me. Even the custom of arranged marriages has been relaxed. They are still arranged, but the kids have a far bigger say in the arranging these days. I don't really have time for girlfriends. People don't believe me when I say that. They think I can get anybody I want. Amir Khan, nice car, big house, loads of money. I'm not like that. My focus is on boxing, winning a world title. There will be plenty of time for that when I'm older. When I go out with my mates we go for something to eat, or something like that. You are more likely to see me in a takeaway than a pub. I don't drink. Bars and clubs are not my scene. Wherever you go there is always trouble with young lads, picking fights and stuff. If I do go to a club, it's usually just to get a mate in. I stay an hour and then come home. The bouncers in Bolton all know me. They are good lads. They make sure nothing happens if I'm around. But they don't see much of me. One night my dad was trying to ring me to see what time I would be coming home. He walked into the room to get his phone and I was in there watching boxing on TV. Besides I have to get up to train. There is always something that needs to be done for my career. I don't feel I have missed out.

At school I never bothered with girls. It was all lads together. It was always boxing, boxing, boxing. It's the same now. I have my goals, and they are all to do with boxing. People come up to me all the time. I talk to them. Girls come up and talk to me. I have a picture taken with them, or something, a laugh and a joke, but nothing serious. The papers have had me going out with a few people, but none of it is true. My mates are always saying that I could have any girl I want. When girls come up to me my mates buzz off it more than I do. I just chill. I know some people in my position chase everything. That's not me.

The way things are now it would be hard to choose the right girl. There will come a time when I settle down, when I finish boxing, say at twenty-six or twenty-seven.

My dad and mum got married the traditional way, by arranged marriage in Pakistan. Then they had a big reception in Bolton at the Spinners' Hall in St George's Road. Everything seems to happen in St George's Road. My sister Tabinda's marriage was arranged too in a loose sense. There is no way she would have married her husband Gohar if she didn't like him. Like Mum and Dad Tabinda had a big do in Matore and then another reception back home in Manchester. That is the route I will probably take. It's cool. I wouldn't mind that. There is no way I would marry someone I did not like, either. You don't get shipped off to Pakistan any more to marry someone you don't know. That's the last thing my family would want. The way it works these days is you choose a girl that you like and vice versa. Marriages are arranged but not without your permission. And they always seem to work out all right. Marrying

In my last year at
Smithills (2002)

Messing about with my
cousin Khalid, Uncle
Taz and cousin Rakeb
(above)
. . . and bodyslamming
Haroon at a family
barbecue (left)

With Uncle Taz
and Dad at the
Junior Olympics
in 2003

Mick Jelley, my mate Majid, Uncle Taz, me, Dad
and my mate Ayaz at the Junior Olympics

© Janis Aukstins

Winning gold and Best Boxer at the European Cadet Championships in Lithuania, 2003, with England team manager Paul King (to my immediate left) and head coach Jim Davidson (to my immediate right)

European Student Championships in Rome in 2003 – an official team shot (above) . . . and a different kind of fighter I met in town (right)

Winning gold and Best Boxer at the Olympic Qualifiers in Bulgaria in 2004 (from left to right): Dad, Taz, me, Tony Davis, my commercial manager Asif Vali, Mick Jelley and Darren Langley

The World Junior Championships in Korea in 2004, where I won the gold medal and Best Boxer award. With coaches Lee Pullin and Chris Edmunds (left) and physio Carolyn who took such good care of my injured hand (below)

Being interviewed at an Olympic sendoff at Bolton's Church Road School, with the mayor of Bolton in the background (above)
My little sister Mariyah chillin' at the Olympic lodge in Athens (below)

Fighting Mario Kindelan in the Olympic final in Athens in 2004

My family and their Union Jacks at the Olympics: Dad, Haroon,
Tabinda, Mariyah, Mum and Uncle Terry

Losing the Olympic
final, with GB coach
Terry Edwards

Having a quick chat with Kindelan before we received our medals

Posing with my Olympic silver medal

All the 2004 Olympic medallists (left to right): me, Kindelan and the two bronze medallists, Khrachev and Yeleuov

for love has never been the done thing in the Asian community. Things are changing. My parents would not force me to do anything. They always say it is up to me. But I am quite happy to do things as they have always been done.

5

Farewell to Kindelan

It was mad after the Olympics. My dad's phone was red hot. I had promoters and trainers contacting me, all wanting to play a part in my career. They all had ideas about what I should do next. There was a lot to think about. I knew that I had a massive decision to make, that I had reached a crossroads. From the moment I started out in boxing, progressed through the amateur ranks, I knew that one day I would turn pro. Getting to Athens instead of Beijing stood everything on its head. It was like a Lottery win. Not in terms of the money on offer, which turned out to be unbelievable, but in terms of my life. It was obvious, even to my eight-year-old sister, that things were not the same as before. Once the dust had settled a bit and everybody had got their breath back, we sat down as a family and tried to work things out.

Mick Jelley was included in the discussions right from the start. He had been with me all the way. He had had other fighters turn pro. Really, he was the only one in the camp who had been at this stage before. But the scale of this was like nothing even he had seen. Mick felt more or less straight away that the time had come to switch codes. He doesn't even like the pro game. He thinks it is a market, where fighters are traded like meat. But he understood the position we were in. When he sat back and thought about what I had achieved he knew I had been massively lucky. The road to the Olympics is so long. There are so many things that can go wrong. Beijing was still four years away. Who was to say that I wouldn't get injured, or catch a cold the night before a qualifier? People have missed flights in the past and not been able to make a bout. What if that happened to me? You only have to look at Wayne Rooney to see how things can strike out of the blue to completely mess up your plans. It almost happened to me at the World Juniors in Korea, when I hurt my thumb. Another mad thing like that might have done for me in Beijing. The more we thought about it, the more we felt blessed to be holding that silver medal.

A few years ago Mick had a lad called Mick Dolan, a light heavyweight. He knocked a kid out in the ABAs. It was on the BBC. A promoter from London saw it and got in touch. Dolan could bang them out. He was no boxer but he was great to watch. The promoter invited him down to London. There was £10,000 on offer and a contract to sign. He said no, I want to win the ABA title first. He made it to the semi-finals. Everything was looking rosy, then he walked on to one, got chinned by a big shot. He was knocked out. He didn't even make the final. That was it. Finished. There was no contract or money on offer for Mick Dolan after that.

Everything happened so quickly to me. A year before going to Athens the Olympics were not even in my thoughts. The next thing I know, I'm in England camps, going to qualifiers. That year passed so quickly I did not have time to think about what was happening to me. I had my Olympic head on and that was it. Now that I had time to reflect a bit, I began to realise just how big a thing it was that I had done. I was gutted about losing out on gold. I thought I was going to do it. Yet judging by the response, all the media attention and the number of letters and emails I received from the public, missing out on gold did not seem to matter to anybody else. The fact that I had made it to an Olympic final at seventeen, and won a medal, was good enough.

How much better could it be coming back with gold in four years, assuming everything went to plan? Besides I had fought the best boxers in the world at the Olympics and in the qualifiers. I had proved myself at that level. I wasn't just winning contests and competitions, I was coming home with best boxer awards. I wasn't sure that I would be stretched any more in the amateurs. On the other hand, I was young. And I wanted to win an ABA senior title. There was the possibility that I might stay amateur for another two years to take me through to the Commonwealth Games. A lot depended on the ABA, and the kind of package they could come up with to allow me to stay amateur. I didn't feel there was any rush to make a decision. My dad did all the talking. I stayed in the background. I had my eye on that ABA senior title to complete the set. I would concentrate on that, keep training and see what happened.

That suited the ABA, who were keen for me to stay amateur as long as possible. They wanted to secure their funding through to the next Olympics. It would not have helped their cause much if I had signed pro immediately. Not in terms of the funding they would soon be getting to take them through to the next major events, but going forward. It is far better for the ABA if they can show continuity. They said they were putting a package together for me. The offer to stay amateur included elite funding of £20,000-odd, tax-free. On top of that the ABA said there would be sponsorship deals to boost that to around £50,000.

Compared to what I had received before the Olympics that was a lot of money. Until I qualified for the Olympics the ABA gave me £10 a week. Once I qualified three months before the Games that went up to £1,200 a month, nowhere near what promoters were coming up with. The first concrete offer I received, other than that from the German promoter Universum, was in Athens. I had just made it to the semi-finals and a guaranteed bronze medal. It was from a British consortium. Six businessmen would put in a total of £1 million. The idea was that I would stay amateur until Beijing. Then when I turned pro after that they would get 50 per cent of my earnings. By then Asif, a friend of the family I knew from way back at Bolton Lads Club, had come on board to help my dad cope with the massive demands. It was getting crazy in Athens. Asif flew in a lawyer, Gareth Williams, to help out, deal with press and media and stuff. It was then that Asif and my dad set up a company called Elite Sports Management. That's how quickly things were happening. A fortnight before going to Athens I was nobody. Then I became the most famous teenager at the Olympic Games. We couldn't wing it any more.

Asif used to sponsor amateur shows at Bury ABC. He had a taxi business in Bolton. My dad used to fix his cars when they broke down. Taxis are a 24/7 business. They didn't break down during office hours, so my dad was more or less on call. They became good friends. Asif started coming to amateur shows. By the time I got to the Olympic qualifiers he was an unofficial part of the family team. It was Asif who took most of the calls in the office when the promoters moved in proper. We said no to the consortium.

My dad came home one day and said, Amir, guess who Asif spoke to today. Go on, who? Oscar De La Hoya. He's been on the phone. He wants you to go and live in the States and fight for him. De La Hoya was the biggest star in world boxing. He had started his own company, Golden Boy Promotions. He wanted me on the books. I felt like I was in Disneyland. De La Hoya was one of my favourite fighters, and he was calling me! Bob Arum, another famous American promoter, made an offer. The only person who didn't seem interested was Don King. He never called. I was flattered. It would have been a buzz to go to America, to try something that had not been done before. It would have been a big step, probably too big at that stage.

I'd been back a few weeks and my dad got a call first thing in the morning from Frank Warren. He wanted to meet. That was the start really. Other leading UK promoters such as Dennis Hobson, Jim Evans and Barry Hearn were also in touch. My dad asked around, spoke to a lot of people. Because we did not know any of the promoters personally, it was difficult to judge. My dad is a down-to-earth man. He ran his yard, but he wasn't a multi-millionaire businessman. He takes people as he finds them. Frank seemed nice enough. As far as we were concerned there was no reason to doubt what he was saying. My dad's main concern was doing the best for his son. He was thinking that it might all end tomorrow. Let's hear what people have to say. My dad and Mick met Frank at the Reebok Stadium in Bolton. Frank basically said what Mick had done, that I was wasting my time going to another Olympics. He felt that it did not make sense in terms of my career or financially to stay on as an amateur. There was just too much that could go wrong. For everything to go according to plan a second time and get to Beijing was a big risk, too big a gamble. Mick went back to the Dolan point. Frank agreed. Strike while the iron is hot, he said. We knew it suited Frank to say that. But it also suited us.

While all this was going on I was back in the ring. Boxing for England against the USA in Liverpool. My opponent was a guy called Michael Evans, who was saying he should have been at Athens representing the USA but missed out for some reason or other, and that he was going to beat me and prove to everyone that he should have been in Athens. As soon as the bell went he came at me but I was too quick for him. Halfway through the first round I caught him with a good right hand and put him on his backside. The ref gave him an eight count and we continued and I eventually beat him on points.

The next time I fought was for the regional ABAs. It was a lot different. I was coming down from international level, the high of Athens. The rings were smaller, the atmosphere different. But I was ready. It made me focus, train harder. I was not going to be taking any chances now. My first bout, my ABA senior debut, was against Craig Watson at the Preston Guildhall. I was trying to please the crowd, my guard was down and I got caught. It was a flash knockdown, good shot, right on the button. It happens in boxing. My legs went, I went down, then got straight back up again. It showed what I was made of. It was a warning if I turned pro. That's how I looked at it. It was also a major news thing on the TV, pictures of me everywhere getting whacked. I recovered to win by a big margin, but no one wanted to talk about that. The Olympic hero was on the seat of his pants. It showed me how quickly things can change, and how a good news story, me winning silver, can easily turn into a bad news story, me on my backside. Everybody wanted to see the big noise brought down to earth. It's natural I suppose. Mick was always telling me this would happen. He was right again. There are a lot of cynical people about who don't like to see you do well.

I had another fight that night against Liam Dorian. He was going to do this, he was going to do that. I was a massive target for these lads. I had never fought in the national seniors before. They were keen to show me what it was all about. Dorian caught me with his shoulder right on the nose, blood everywhere, like a tap. It was the first time anybody had really drawn blood from me. I've been whacked on the nose loads of times and nothing. After that for a few days you only had to flick it and blood came pouring out. It didn't stop me beating him by a big margin. I was through to the North-west finals in Liverpool. I fought a lad called Steve Williams. Again, no problem, I stopped him on the twenty-points rule. The venues were all packed, sold out.

Next up was the ABA quarter-finals in Great Yarmouth. I was really looking forward to it. I was just three fights from picking up my first senior title in England. After the Williams fight, Asif went for a drink with Paul King of the ABA. Paul knew there was a ticket problem in Yarmouth. The ABA had promised us a few hundred tickets. All the shows were selling out. People wanted to see this young star from the Olympics. The amateur scene was buzzing off it. Good luck for the tickets in Yarmouth, Paul said. Asif looked puzzled. What do you mean, good luck with the tickets? You might get three or four. Any more than that and I'd be surprised.

Asif rang Great Yarmouth. The officials confirmed what Paul King had said. You can have ten tickets. It's the same for all the fighters. If we get any back, we'll let you know. Asif was fuming. My dad went mad. It was starting to get really heavy. There was only two weeks to go before the fight. People had to make arrangements. Asif told them about the promise the ABA had made over tickets. It's nothing to do with the ABA, they said. It's our show. We'll organise it how we like. Asif could not believe it. They would not give an inch. They had made it a dinner show. That meant higher ticket prices, more money for them. Asif asked them to change the venue. They refused. We went back to Paul King. Sorry, he said. It's out of my hands. I was shocked. Why were they doing this to us? Why were they treating us this way? They were selling tickets on the back of my Olympic success and were not prepared to give us any to sell to all the people in the North-west who wanted to support me in the ABAs. We did not have any problems in Preston or Liverpool. We were given 200 to 300 tickets there and sold them all, no problem.

At one of the schoolboy championships I fought at in London there was loads of trouble over tickets. They did not let the fighters have enough. A lot of people wanted to see their kids fight and could not get in. Riot police turned up, dog handlers, vans, the lot. They ended up cancelling the show because of safety. It was a right mess. Frightening. I was scared that the same thing would happen in Great Yarmouth. I did not want to be held responsible for another riot like that. I would be the one mentioned on TV, in news reports, riots at Amir Khan show.

My dad and Asif sat me down, explained the seriousness of the situation, asked me what I wanted to do. I was close to tears, very emotional. I had set my heart on this. I'd won the World Juniors, Olympic silver. This was different. It was the ABAs. Coming through the ranks, the ABAs are massive. I wanted the title. I was also angry, as mad as I have ever been in boxing. The ABA had the power to help. They chose not to. That hurt. I had a lump in my throat. I felt I had no choice. It felt personal, like they were trying to take the opportunity away from me. I thought I deserved better after all I had done for amateur boxing in this country. They showed me no respect. I told my dad that if they would not give us the tickets I'd pull out.

My dad rang Paul King. He told him that unless something changed, I was pulling out. Paul said he would ring back by four that afternoon. Four o'clock came and went. At 5 p.m. we rang the Press Association and told them that Amir Khan had pulled out of the ABAs. There was no turning back. At 5.30 p.m. my dad took a call from London. It was the ABA. They said they had got us 300 tickets. It was too late. As my dad put it at the time, if they could find 300 tickets half an hour after I pulled out, why couldn't they do it half an hour before? My dad stuck to his guns. I was not going to fight.

The next forty-eight hours were bedlam. Lots of media interest, live interviews on the radio. The ABA tried to rectify the situation. They came up with the idea of letting me box in the afternoon of the main show. No chance. I felt betrayed by the ABA. I feel the same way now. They did nothing for us. We found out later that the lad I was supposed to be fighting in Great Yarmouth had broken his hand. There was never going to be a fight because I would have been given a bye into the semi-finals, so all the fuss was about nothing. Nobody told us. They must have known that if they released the news that I wasn't fighting, it would hit ticket sales.

Despite all that, we attended the finals. The ABA were presented with a cheque for over £1 million at the finals, funding for the next Olympics. That was money I had helped them to get, and they did nothing for me when it mattered. It left a bitter taste. Still does. I had to fight for everything I ever got out of the ABA, to go to the qualifiers, the Worlds. Everything was a battle. That was a big factor in my decision to turn pro. There was one more thing that helped tip me over the edge, the fight with Mario Kindelan.

After the ABA finals there was a match coming up, Great Britain versus Cuba. That would have allowed me another crack at Kindelan. It was a fight everybody wanted to see. We asked the ABA to put me in against him. They said they couldn't because I had not won the senior ABA title. Again the ABA were trying to block me. The fact that I was the Olympic silver medallist did not mean a thing. Rules are rules. Kindelan ended up fighting Frankie Gavin instead. He didn't get out of first gear. He beat Frankie easily. After that the Cubans were going to Ireland. We knew Kindelan wouldn't fight in Ireland so we asked the ABA to keep him in England and put him on a Bury ABC show against me. We had a date available. My dad spoke to Paul King. Paul said the ABA couldn't do it. The Irish would not release him. As we expected Kindelan didn't fight in Ireland.

At this point Frank Warren was involved. He had been in constant touch with Dad and Asif while the ABA fiasco was going on. He offered to help in any way he could to get a fight on with Kindelan. We had another date available for the end of April, two weeks away. My dad suggested to the ABA that they keep Kindelan in England when the Cubans got back from Ireland. We would meet all his expenses. It would not cost the ABA a penny. No, they said. He has to go back to Cuba to fight in the Cuban championships so he can't make the 30 April date. That might have been the case but, for me, the ABA was just changing the goal posts, blocking me again. They did not want this fight to happen. We cancelled the April date.

We came up with another date, 14 May. Frank was leading the negotiations with the ABA now. Finally the ABA agreed to the new date. The Cubans would come back. I'd get my fight with Kindelan. It was all I could think about now. I wanted to show the world I could beat him. A few days before the fight, Frank gets a call. There were no visas. The Cubans had not got visas. The ABA were supposed to organise everything. Nothing had been done. Frank's partner Ed Simons went to work. He was on to the Cuban embassy day and night. He was speaking to people in Havana and London to try to get the visas sorted out. At the last minute the call came through. Ed had got the visas. Kindelan was coming over.

I was buzzing. The show was billed as an England versus Cuba match at the Reebok Stadium, the only time I fought as an amateur within the boundaries of Bolton. My dad rang up Paul King again to make sure of the arrangements. What time do they arrive? In the morning, Paul said. Great, who's picking them up from the airport? How are they getting to Bolton? We thought you were picking them up, said Paul. This was all supposed to be happening the next day. My dad and Asif were stunned. They had to hire a minibus and drive down to Gatwick themselves to collect Kindelan and the rest of the Cuban team. There was only one ABA official to greet them, Billy Phillips. Dad brought them up to Bolton and put them up at the De Vere Hotel at the Reebok. That didn't come cheap, either. The ABA did not pay a penny for the minibus or the hotel. That did not stop them taking a cut of the money ITV paid to televise the show.

The Kindelan thing was the last straw for me and Dad. We had had it with the ABA. Frank Warren had impressed us with the help he had given us to get the Kindelan fight. Without the work Ed Simons did, it would never have happened. The offer that the ABA had promised to put together to take me through to the Commonwealths never materialised. Asif kept asking for a formal proposal. Nothing.

Promoters, on the other hand, were very busy behind the

scenes. We were not aware at the time but, looking back, TV was crucial to the way things turned out. All the big players were coming to the end of their deals with promoters, the BBC, ITV and Sky. Asif approached the BBC to try to do a deal direct. They were not interested. They felt that they had had their fingers burned with Audley Harrison. They did not want another commercial deal with a fighter in that way. They would be doing a deal with the ABA to stage amateur bouts and if I were staying amateur that would be great for everybody.

We knew that ITV were interested in doing something when they chose to broadcast what turned out to be my last fight as an amateur against Kindelan. We knew that whatever promoter signed me up would get a deal with ITV or with one of the other major broadcasters.

All of the promoters were jockeying for position, however Frank impressed us the most. Before I signed my dad and Asif asked a lot of people about Frank. What was clear was that at this stage in my career, Frank was the best person for me. Even Naseem Hamed, who Frank had had a public falling out with a number of years ago, confirmed this.

We talked it through. My dad was impressed with the way Frank ran his business, his contacts, the help and support he had given and his plans for me. After all he had been in this position before, set up the career of Hatton from scratch and built the careers of Hamed and Calzaghe after they had started with other promoters. Frank's wasn't even the best offer. Dennis Hobson offered more. And at the last minute Barry Hearn came in with a mega deal, way better than the rest. It didn't matter. My dad met with Frank and Ed Simons, Frank's business partner, at Marble Arch in London a week before the Kindelan fight After negotiating hard, he shook hands on a deal then. That was it. My dad does not say a lot but once he gives you his word, there is no turning back.

We signed in Manchester the day before the Kindelan fight. It was after the press conference with Hatton before his big show with Kostya Tszyu. We were in the Midland Hotel. When Frank had finished with the Hatton conference we went to another room. There was no big fuss. It was really quiet, just me, Dad, Asif, Frank, my uncle Taz, Mick and the lawyers. We sat round a table, chatted a bit, spoke about the future. Then the papers were put in front of me. They showed me where to sign. I didn't read the contract. I knew what was in it. I knew what it meant. I put pen to paper. It was a brilliant moment. That one signature changed my life. I had earned my first wage. It was a big thing for me. Massive. Everybody shook hands, I hugged my dad. It was done.

We went back to Bolton. There was no great celebration. I was preparing for my pro debut. We just chilled, had some food. The funny thing was, we didn't really speak about the money much. All I could think about was being a professional boxer. All I had ever known was the amateurs. It would be like starting over again in a new job. In the amateurs I was the top man. I had my team behind me. Everybody knew about me. I was used to running the show. Now I was out on my own. I had to learn things all over again. It felt really strange.

Before that, I had one last thing to do as an amateur, beat Kindelan. My dad had kept me away from the negotiations with Frank. My focus was on preparing for the fight. Or trying to. One day it was on, the next it was off. When I heard he was finally on a flight from Cuba, it was brilliant. The hype was massive. There were posters all over Bolton. Everywhere people went, I was staring down at them. The atmosphere in the town was fantastic. It was like Bolton had reached the FA Cup Final. I felt like I was making history. This was a grudge match, the biggest fight of my career, definitely. I wanted to show who was the best. This would be my last fight as an amateur. Other than my family and Frank Warren, no one knew that. Not even Terry Edwards, who had been in my corner the last time I fought Kindelan at the Olympics.

It was weird being in Bolton, knowing Kindelan was in a hotel just around the corner. I heard that he was training, that he looked in great shape. That was good. I didn't want anybody to think he was just going through the motions. This was his last fight, too. He did not want to retire a loser. I had seen him against Frankie Gavin the month before. I knew I could get him. I had been training really hard for the fight. For the first time as an amateur I was able to train to fight one way. At the Olympics and other major tournaments I had to dedicate time to all different styles. You never knew what you would get. This time I knew. Kindelan was a southpaw. All my training was based on that, facing a lefty. I could see he was confident. He must have been thinking that I was still only a kid. He'd already beaten me twice. He had not lost a fight for six or seven years. It was important not to lose now. He was a hero in Cuba, a legend everywhere else. Fighters like Kindelan don't like to lose. Since the fight people like Michael Grant have been critical, saying it was obvious Kindelan wasn't trying to win. Crap. He was ready.

So was I. I watched video after video, day after day. Mentally, I had been preparing for this night since the Olympics. I wanted to show that I was the best amateur in the world. I wanted to shut everyone up, all those who questioned me, who thought I could never beat him, all those who thought I was mad to take the fight. In my mind it was definitely the biggest fight of my career.

On the night of the fight I had booked a room in the hotel opposite his. I got there early. I started to feel a bit peckish so, about two hours before I was due in the ring, I nipped out for a McDonald's with a couple of mates. I had a fillet of fish and a sugar cake. It helped take my mind off things. We had a laugh for a bit. I went back to the hotel on my own. For the last hour I was on my own. No mates. This was it. I went into fight mode.

About an hour or so before the bout we entered the ring

together, me and Kindelan. We exchanged gifts. That was the only time I actually saw him before the fight. Then it was into the changing room. Get my hands taped. The usual rituals. He was called into the ring first. The people clapped him in. That pleased me. It is sport. Mick drilled that into us from the start. It's about respect. I was glad that the crowd, my fans, showed their respect for Kindelan, a great fighter.

When I left the changing room I had cameras following me. I could see how massive the fight was. Bolton manager Sam Allardyce, England cricket hero Freddie Flintoff, boxer Nigel Benn, people like that, were in the crowd. I was nervous, excited. Everyone stood as I got close to the ring. I noticed a big poster of Kindelan. My heart was pumping. Security were pushing people away, keeping them back. Everybody was cheering, shouting my name. Those close enough to me tried to reach out to touch me, pat me on the back. I climbed into the ring, always a special moment. I could see people, people I knew. Yet at the same time I couldn't see anybody. I was in the zone. The referee called us over. We exchanged signed pictures. Back to the corners. The bell went.

I thought he would start slow, throw a few sneaky shots to the body. I was on my toes, in and out. I didn't want to rush in. He likes that. It gives him a target. At the Olympics he used that to his advantage. He was expecting me to fight that way. He had worked me out big time in Athens and I did not have the experience to turn things around quickly enough. This was different. I had worked him out. I knew how he wanted me to fight. That threw him. I was a point up after the first round. Technically, everything went like clockwork.

At the Olympics I was also a point ahead after one round. I got carried away, came out blazing in the second, walked right into Kindelan's trap. This time I kept the pace exactly the same, nice and technical. It was like a game of chess, only this time I was dictating terms, making the first moves. My footwork was great.

I caught him with a couple of good shots. That gave me confidence. Two points up at halfway.

In the third round I could see he was getting tired. I upped the pace, caught him with a cracking combination. I threw a right hand, a left hook and another right. The last one missed but I could see he was hurt. I had never seen him hurt like that before. I caught him flush on the chin with that first right hand. He grabbed and held. I could have rushed in. I didn't. I stayed calm, stepped back, threw the jab. In and out. On my toes. The bell went. I was four points up and buzzing. Two minutes from victory.

In the fourth I knew he would come out strong. I knew what to do. Hit and move, let him come on to me. At the Games I was down going into the fourth. I would rush in and he would step to the side, hit and move. Here it was Kindelan who needed to catch up. He couldn't find me. He was getting more and more frustrated. He charged in, threw a punch, missed. He grabbed hold of me and just laughed. That was the moment that I knew I had the great Kindelan beat. I caught him with some good shots, great shots. The bell went.

It was the greatest feeling. I knew this was going to be my final amateur bout. I wanted to finish as one of the best amateurs this country had ever seen. English lads don't beat Cubans, especially top-class Cubans like Kindelan. It never happens. That is what I did. I beat Mario Kindelan.

The next few days were a blur. I announced immediately that I was turning pro. Five days later there was a press conference to announce the date of my first professional fight, 16 July 2005 in Bolton. Frank switched the heavyweight fight between Danny Williams and Matt Skelton from London to the Bolton Arena. I was on the undercard.

There was a lot to take in, a lot to learn. The pro game is completely different. More than anything it meant meeting new people, forming new relationships. Everything I had ever known as an amateur was behind me, a bit like changing schools or starting university. I was the new boy. I knew nothing. I was very conscious of that in those first few days.

At the same time it was incredibly exciting. I was a rich lad for one thing. I didn't know anything about money. I had never had any of my own. I'd gone straight from school, almost, to being a very wealthy lad. I was clueless. Money was not my motivation. When we sat down with the bank manager to arrange an allowance, she asked how much I would like a week, £50, £100, £500, £1,000. When I said ten, she said fine, £10,000 it is. I couldn't spend that in a year. She laughed when I said ten quid, I'm not a big spender. Shall we round that up to £50? she said.

The money was nice. I wouldn't deny that. I was able to make my family comfortable. I was proud to do that at eighteen. I sat down with my mum and dad, my uncles, the people who had made it possible for me to achieve what I did. When they were travelling up and down the country with me to amateur shows, we never thought that one day we would be in this position. It was nice to be able to give something back, my way of saying thank you. I also gave myself a little treat. A Range Rover Vogue. I was hunting around for deals. I wanted a car that would fit the whole family in, my brother and sisters and stuff. There are six of us. I bought it from a local garage, very exciting. It was top of the range, a lot of money. No one had a car like it in Bolton before. I couldn't even drive. I had to put L-plates on it. No one ever put L-plates on a Range Rover in Bolton before. Check that out. Amir Khan in a Range Rover. I loved it. I had loads of extras put in it, heated seats, alloy wheels, base boxes, PlayStation, satellite stuff. That came to more than £10,000. I didn't pay that. I did a picture for a magazine selling that kind of gear. That's all they wanted, one picture of me to use in their magazine. I remember driving in it to my first pro fight. It felt brilliant pulling into the car park.

When I passed my test in November 2005 I let my dad have the Range Rover and bought a present for myself. A BMW Schnitzer convertible, leather seats, electric everything, and quick. That's some car for anyone, never mind a teenager.

6

Punching for Pay

The relationship between a boxer and his trainer is one of the most important in sport. You spend a lot of time in a small, enclosed space with the same guy so you have to make sure that you get on, that you like each other, respect each other. I knew from my amateur days how tricky it could be when I moved on to the international stage and had to work with the England coaches as opposed to Mick at Bury. The things that you had been used to, the little rituals that you relied on went out of the window. At international level it is often those little things that make the difference. I always felt better when I knew Mick was in the arena, if I could see him on my way to the ring, even if he could not be in my corner.

The process that led to working with Mick was different from choosing a trainer as a pro. At eleven I did as I was told and accepted what was put in front of me. In that sense I was lucky that Mick and I got along well. I accepted his authority, did exactly as I was told. That worked for Mick. He didn't like cheeky kids. He would not have stood for the tearaway I used to be. As I only lost twice as an amateur when Mick was in my corner that tells you how well we worked together. I had nothing against the England coaches. They all knew their stuff. It was just that Mick knew my ways, how I did things. He could read my mood and never tried to mould me into something I could never be. Some of the international coaches had a rigid understanding of how a young boxer should fight. Mick was more relaxed about things as long as the fundamentals were in place.

By the time I had signed on the dotted line with Frank in Manchester the hardest part had been decided. I would be working with Oliver Harrison. Initially I was looking for someone to work with for the Kindelan fight in Bolton. If that went well then we would see. I had spoken to other trainers on the phone and been to a couple of gyms. There was no shortage of interest. Location was always going to be important. Whoever I chose to go with would have to be in striking distance of Bolton. So that meant someone based in Manchester.

We put a call in to Frank to seek his input. He had experience of all the Manchester trainers over the years: Brian Hughes, who had the likes of Robin Reid, good fighters, and Billy Graham, who had a string of top pros, notably Ricky Hatton. We spoke to Robbie on the phone. He was telling me how good it was with Brian. Brian is a nice bloke, a boxing man through and through. But it was not for me. I went over to Ricky's gym to see how it worked with Billy. That was good. They are great people but something about it didn't feel quite right. The atmosphere didn't suit me. It suited Ricky down to the ground, but I was looking for something a bit different. I couldn't spell it out. It was just a feeling. Boxing intuition.

Frank suggested Oliver. Leave it with me, he said. I'll sort something out. Oliver was with Jamie Moore in Germany at the time. Jamie was working as a sparring partner over there. Oliver is very particular about his phones. He has two mobiles, one for business, one personal for his friends. That way he can screen his calls. If he does not recognise the number or the name, he doesn't answer it. He recognised Frank's all right. The conversation went something like this.

F: Oliver, it's Frank.

O: Hello, Frank, how can I help?

F: Where are you?

O: In Germany.

F: What are you doing there?

O: I'm with Jamie Moore. He's doing a bit of sparring over here.

F: Oliver, with the greatest respect, you don't need to be there with Jamie Moore sparring. You can get someone else to take care of that. I need you over here to talk with the Khan people about the training of Amir Khan. Maybe you should get a plane over here right now.

To his credit Oliver wasn't sure what to do at first. His responsibility was to his fighter. He understood the significance of the call. Frank doesn't phone in the middle of the day to do small talk. He knew also that he wasn't really being asked, he was being told. And it was a fantastic opportunity. Olympic silver medallists do not come along every day. I don't want that to sound big-headed. But that is how you have to see it. That is how Oliver saw it. Oliver put his mobile on loudspeaker. He did not want to hide anything from Jamie. In the end Jamie made the decision for him. Oliver, he said, you had better get that ticket, go home and get it sorted. As Oliver told me later, he can think of a lot of other fighters who would have responded in a different way. That's the kind of lad Jamie is. He's a top bloke, and a good fighter. Jamie used to be on Frank's books. He's moved on now but there are no hard feelings.

Oliver came over. We met and pretty much hit it off straight away. I can tell immediately if a coach is any good or not. After that it is a question of how well you get on. We got on well from the off. We must have watched videos of the Kindelan fight at the Olympics a thousand times. His analysis was brilliant. He was great on the pads too. The way he held them, the style he talked about. All of this hit the spot with me. Speed and power you more or less develop yourself. You can improve them for sure, but you can't make a weak man strong through technique or a slow man quick.

I liked the fact that Oliver involved me in decisions. It was not just one-way traffic. You need a coach who understands your point of view, your side of the story. Oliver would make suggestions. Then he would ask me what I thought I should be doing to beat Kindelan. Mick was the same in the early days, and when I started boxing in the seniors with Terry, he would always talk things through as a team. For this bout Oliver was happy to pick my brains. I was the one who had fought Kindelan twice. I was the only one who knew how hard he punched, how he moved, who saw the whites of his eyes close up. It was a respect thing. Oliver was giving me as much respect as I was giving him. There isn't a coaching manual that tells you about these things. Any experienced coach can tell you how to throw a left hook, how to step to the left, to jab and stuff. Coaching at elite level is more about relationships than anything else.

There were enough experts out there who thought I would not beat Kindelan in my last amateur fight. Colin Hart, who as boxing correspondent of the *Sun* saw all the great fighters from Muhammad Ali and Joe Frazier to the present day, said to Oliver that I could not beat Kindelan. Before I went to the Olympics Colin did not believe I would win a medal. He said as much in his column. Afterwards he was big enough to apologise. Oliver was confident of the outcome and told Colin that.

We kept my involvement with Oliver quiet. I was technically still an amateur. Mick and Terry were my official trainers for the Kindelan fight, they were the ones in my corner on the night. Terry did not know anything about Oliver at that stage. He got on with the job as he would for any other international bout. We went down to training camp in Portsmouth. In fact we had two or three camps. I loved it. But at the same time I felt a bit uncomfortable about keeping him in the dark. There should not be any secrets between fighter and trainer. But there was a lot going on behind the scenes with the ABA and with Frank about turning pro. Things were on a knife edge. Terry was an employee of the ABA so it was better for him that he didn't know what was going on. It was like a rite of passage. I was moving from boy to man. I was becoming part of the decision-making in a way that I had not been before. I had to start taking responsibility for a few things. Keeping a secret from Terry was one of those responsibilities. I had to do it.

Terry probably guessed what was going on. He's been around the game a long time. He actually found out for certain on the night of the Kindelan fight. After my win, Frank was interviewed on the TV. Though he had done so much to make the Kindelan fight happen and had done the deal with ITV by then, he was committed to a function in London on the same night. He couldn't make it to the Reebok Stadium. In the interview he announced that the Kindelan fight was my last as an amateur. Terry happened to be watching. In an ideal world I would have told him. That's life.

It didn't affect our relationship. We are still in touch. After fights he rings me up sometimes and threatens to get the pet out. The pet was a boxing glove on a piece of string. Whenever I carried my hands too low, Terry would whack me with the pet. It was a good lesson.

In that respect professional boxing is no different from amateur boxing. You get punished just the same in both codes if your hands are by your sides. I was itching to get on with things after the Kindelan fight. The date for my first professional fight was announced fairly soon. I had six weeks to prepare.

You wouldn't call Langley Road in Salford a beauty spot. At the top end as you turn in you pass a crematorium and cemetery. That is the best bit. After that the road takes you into old Manchester. Scrub that. Old Salford. If you ever refer to Salford as Manchester there is a fair chance you will end up in the crematorium. Salford people are proud of their city, just as we are in Bolton. The gym is only about eight miles from home. My dad used to drive me down. I hadn't passed my test at that stage. After the cemetery it starts to get very bleak, lots of old industrial warehouses and units. On the left as you approach the gym there is a sandwich shop that keeps the workers in bacon butties. I've never tried one myself. As a Muslim I don't eat pork. On the right down a side street opposite the gym is the Beehive pub. That's about it for local landmarks.

If you didn't know what you were looking for you would never find the gym. There is a small sign saying Oliver's Gym on a massive brick wall on the opposite side of the road. That is not much use for first-time visitors. People think the gym is either behind the wall or directly opposite. Behind the wall is a big industrial yard. Opposite is a school. The only giveaway is a sign on the front of what looks like a disused building saying Salford kick boxing club. Even then you would struggle to work out what was going on because the two doors on that side of the building are hidden behind massive steel plates. You would need dynamite to shift them. The entrance is actually around the other side, hidden from the main road. Lots of people go to gyms these days. I do a lot of press and media stuff at Virgin Active in Bolton. The facilities are brilliant, state-of-the-art stuff. Nice showers, TV screens, a place to sit and have coffee. That's what I thought a professional gym might be like. Oliver's Gym is the opposite of that. In fact it is no better than the first gym I walked into, the old Halliwell Club in Bolton.

That's what I liked about it. There is not much to it, really. And what there is looks like it's falling apart. A small entrance area leads you to a big floor space about the size of a badminton court with weights at one end. A door on the left of the back wall leads into a smaller room. Inside are two boxing rings set in opposite corners with just enough room to pass between the two.

In another corner there is an old running machine, a speed ball and a few bags. Everything is old and battered and damp. I love it like that. You don't want some posh place with high-tech stuff, all polished. You have to go in there and hit someone. The last corner, where the door is, is free. That is where Oliver rigs up the dreaded bag bar, a rusty old thing about two metres long. I hate that bar. Everybody does. The bar, supported at each end, is raised almost one metre off the floor, about the height of an office desk. Jumping over that with your knees and ankles together is the hardest thing you can do. It absolutely kills you. The walls are full of old posters. It's cheaper than decorating. Mike Tyson has to share pride of place with local Manchester fighters. The most important bit of kit is the ghetto blaster. That sets the tone, the rhythm of the place.

Jamie Moore is one of the big characters in the gym. Jamie took to me straight away. There is a lot of jealousy in sport. Boxing is no different. When a young lad comes along with a big contract and an Olympic medal, it can cause a bit of upset. It has never been a problem for Jamie or the rest of the lads in the gym. It's only a small stable. Intimate. That's what I was looking for. One-on-one coaching with my trainer. For a spell Andrew Flintoff used to use the gym. It's not the sort of place you would expect to find an England cricketer going through his paces. Then again Flintoff is not your average England cricketer. Jamie brought him along. They're good mates. He's not been down lately. Maybe the England captaincy went to his head. Only joking, Freddie.

Atmosphere is everything. Oliver won't have any negative influences in the gym. It's the one bad apple thing. One moody lad can ruin it for everybody. Oliver treats everybody the same. He knows that on one level I'm a special case, a celebrity if you like. The Olympics made me famous. But being known by millions was never going to make me a better fighter. Oliver could not give a monkey's about the celebrity bit. He even turned down an invite to visit Mike Tyson in his room when he was staying in the Midland Hotel in Manchester. He reckoned that if Iron Mike wanted to see him, the man who trains Amir Khan, he would come around to the gym. Tyson never made it.

The way Oliver sees it, I suit him as much as he suits me. If it were not a two-way thing it would not work. Oliver did not want to train me the way others thought it should be done. He recognised that I was not made to be standing in front of a body bag for hours on end, bang, bang, bang, then jumping into the ring for more of the same. He wanted to maintain the style I had, to use the skills that I had developed, the speed and movement, not sacrifice them for power and durability. Not everybody throws a left hook in the same way. You can't mould fighters. You have to make subtle adjustments. Oliver's background was Thai boxing. He started off as a kid with boxing but moved to Thai boxing when he was fifteen. He won a world title then tried to make the switch to pro boxing. He found out that without a proper manager and promoter you have next to no chance of making it. Oliver was part of the Champs Camp gym run by Phil Martin in Manchester. Champs Camp was really where the Manchester boxing revival started. When Phil died, Billy Graham set up his own gym training the likes of Ensley Bingham, Carl Thompson and Steve Foster.

The first thing Oliver and I did was some work on the pads. There was no one else in the gym. Later on we did a media workout. It was jam-packed with radio and TV people. On this occasion we were on our own. The pads tell you how a boxer punches, what angles he likes, his strength and power. Oliver would ask me how I liked the pads to be held. Stuff like that. In the early stages as a pro it's all about making the right adjustments. As an amateur you tend to be on your toes more, in and out, tippy tappy stuff. That's how you score points, win bouts. You are not trying to knock out an opponent. You are trying to beat him by landing more scoring shots. As a pro you have to be prepared to stand and trade a bit more, to take a shot to throw a shot. If you stuck with an amateur strategy, your opponent would just walk straight through you. It's not easy to make the transition. Lots of successful amateur boxers have found it difficult to adapt.

We were working on conserving energy, slowing my feet down a bit. At times even staying flat-footed. By planting your feet you anchor the legs. That is where pros get their power from, by gripping the canvas with the toes almost. It's a completely different technique. In the amateurs you are swinging from the hip more. In the pros the punch starts in the sole of your boot. When you connect you can feel a kind of charge right from the knuckle at the point of impact all the way up your arm into your shoulder. It's a bit like hitting a cricket shot off the middle of the bat. It's in the timing. And like hitting a four through the covers it gives you the sweetest feeling.

We worked on planting the feet a bit more and getting the punches right with the turning of the wrist. That gives you your snap. That took some time. I was a quick learner. I was hungry. I knew that the people I would be fighting would see me as a scalp. It would be their big chance, their big payday. At the end of my time in the amateurs everybody knew who I was. People were always trying to avoid me. In the pros it was the opposite. These lads were desperate for a shot.

Dean Powell is the man responsible for scouring the country for the right opponent. Dean is one of the great characters in boxing, pin thin with a bald head and piercing eyes. He comes from the Midlands and his accent is thicker than mine. Dean has taken over from the late Ernie Fosse, another great boxing character who was with Frank a long time. Dean chats it through with Frank, then my dad and Oliver have their input. We have not turned down one opponent yet. Matchmaking is critical. If you pitch a novice too high too early it can end his career. Too low and everybody starts moaning saying you are fighting hand-picked opponents. My dad has posted the records of a few top fighters on my website so that people can compare my early opponents with theirs. Muhammad Ali's record is up there. So is Naseem Hamed's and Lennox Lewis's.

David Bailey was the name Dean picked out of the hat for my first fight. He had a fifty-fifty record, which was about right. And for the first time in my boxing life I had an opponent saying he was going to knock me out, to take my head off. That was all new to me. He was telling me how it was a new ball game now. And I was in the wrong game. Before I had seen boxing as a sport. You didn't say that sort of stuff. Mick would never have allowed it. You had to respect your opponent. We didn't really do mind games. All the talk made me more determined to be right. It was my first fight. I did not want any mistakes.

Once Oliver had worked out my style on the pads the priority was to get me fit, to build stamina. That meant the bag bar. That special piece of torture equipment goes back to the old Phil Martin days at Champs Camp. It is the same thing Ricky Hatton does with Billy Graham. It's murder. One minute on the bar, one minute on the bag, back on the bar and a minute to recover. You build it up from there. After that first time I was nearly dead. I felt like my heart was falling out. It's vital preparation. In the amateurs you are fighting four two-minute rounds. In the pros each round lasts three minutes. You have to be ready for that. It was hard at first. I was knackered. It was a long time since I'd felt like that. After the bar you are straight on the bag. You feel like death but you have to hit the bag. One day you will throw a ten-punch combination and your opponent will still be stood there saying, come on, let's go. Is that all you've got? When you reach that point you have to start throwing punches all over again and move. That's what the bar is for, to prepare you for that day. If you can't throw punches in that kind of situation you are going to get whacked yourself. You give up in your mind first. If your mind is strong you can push your body through the pain barrier. That's what you have to do to win, go further than the other fella. That's just what it was like against the Romanian lad in the Olympic qualifiers. He kept coming forward. You want to stop. Your body is screaming for you to do just that. You have to send a different message back to your brain. Pride and adrenalin keep you going. I wanted to win that bout so badly. I would never give up. That was only a four-rounder. In the pros you learn to pace yourself, conserve your energy. All that bouncing around you do as an amateur just saps energy that you might need for the later rounds.

So fitness had to be there. I built up my fitness so that I could work for three or four minutes at a time on the pads. If you can work that long on the pads, you can do it in the ring. Lots of boxers would prefer to spar, risk getting whacked, than go on the pads. I don't mind them. Every now and then Oliver will force me through a really tough session, throwing up to 450 punches. You might throw about seventy in a round during a fight. The one advantage novice pros have is energy. Pros tend to get lazy. It's inevitable after so long. Making the weight and training gets to be a real drag. I've not suffered any of that. I have to eat extra portions of pizza rather than starve myself to make the 63-kilo weight limit.

I used the same sparring partner for the first fight as I did for the Kindelan bout in Bolton. He's a Nigerian kid called Mo. If he has a second name, nobody knows it. He's good, a tough lad with a head you could break rocks on. Working with Mo for 3-minute rounds gave me confidence. I knew if I could go four rounds with him I would have no trouble with Bailey.

There was another dimension to the pro game that I had not had to deal with as an amateur. Press conferences. I did them at the Olympics after fights, but not before. Most novice pros would not expect to do them either. They can enjoy a bit of anonymity.

It was different with me. That silver medal at seventeen turned everything on its head. I was one of the best-known boxers in the country and I had not even had a pro fight. There was a lot resting on it. I found facing the press mentally draining. You get used to it eventually. You learn that it is something you have to put up with. I would still much rather do a training session on the bag and bar than do a press conference but I'm OK with it now. It was all so new before my debut. I understood after the Olympics that it is the response of people to you rather than the other way around that changes. As far as I was concerned I was just another lad in the gym. To others I was this famous person and they treated me accordingly. It was mad.

Like everything else I tried to turn it to my advantage. I wasn't going to let the attention go to my head. If anything the opposite was true. It motivated me to train harder. I knew people were waiting for me to fall on my face. I was never going to give them the satisfaction. I was going to be as good as I could be against Bailey. By instinct, that is the attitude I have always had. As a fighter it keeps me honest.

Bailey talked a good fight. He was this former British Thai boxing champion who had had seven pro fights. I was just an amateur boxer. He was going to teach me a lesson, show me what professional boxing was all about. He would have to be in the best shape of his life to do that because I was in the best shape of mine.

The town was buzzing. The whole day was electric. My dad's phone never stopped, texts, messages. Some from people he did not even know. I was relaxed. More quiet than normal, perhaps, but confident. In the amateurs there were never any doubts. Mick would come round to the house, we'd jump in the car and set off. No problem. I knew what to expect when I got there and was always super confident about the result. This was a bit different. My first pro fight. It was special. It meant something to a lot of people.

I had an early night as usual. I stayed in bed on the morning of the fight, got up about half past ten. Then got my kit together. I just tried to relax, really. As the fight neared we just waited for the phone call to make our way in. It was all done to order to suit the television schedule. We were working around them, which was new. Everything had to run like clockwork. You had to be there at a certain time to do a piece to camera before the fight. It was a big production. The TV people take over in a way. Whether you are ready or not, whether it suits you or it doesn't, you have to be there when they want you.

We didn't live far from the venue, about a mile and a half. I drove in with Dad. Just me and him. We left the house about 6.45 p.m. The street was quiet. It was like a normal Saturday night in Bolton at that point. I just threw my kit in the back of the car and climbed in as if we were going to Tesco. As we got into Horwich, the traffic started to build. Lots of police cars and stuff. When we arrived at the De Vere Hotel in the Reebok Stadium the crowds were massive. It was like a big football match. There were some roadworks on the dual carriageway that meant we had to go as far as the Blackrod roundabout then come back on ourselves. We passed a footbridge outside the station near the arena. It was full of people walking to the event. My dad started to get emotional. He's like that. He filled up. He did not think it would be so big. All these people had turned up to see his son. It was the Olympics, the Kindelan fight all over again. I was focused. I was thinking only of the fight, of getting in that ring and doing my stuff. You can't let things get to you. It spoils your rhythm.

There was no McDonald's that night. I was due in the ring about 9.30 p.m. I had a bit of music playing in the changing room. Oliver was in there with me, Jed his no. 2, my dad, my mate Saj, my brother. Asif kept coming in and out. Mick the same.

In the amateurs all the fighters get changed together in the same room. You know your bout number so you can tell when you are going on. Bout no. 6, Amir Khan, and away you go. This was totally different. I was waiting for some bloke from ITV to pop his head around the corner to give us the nod. Two minutes, he said. That was it.

My dad went out just before me. Everyone was on their feet. David Bailey went out first. Then I walked into the arena. 'Amarillo' was booming out of the sound system. The place erupted. It was banged out. Big Sam Allardyce was there again with a few of the Bolton backroom lads. All my friends, my college mates, everyone I knew from Bolton. I've never really boxed in front of a crowd like that in Bolton. The Kindelan fight was a dinner show, nowhere near as many people could get in to that. This time everybody was there. The noise was unbelievable. I was nervous. I did not know what to expect. I prepared well, trained hard. I knew that I was ready to fight but I was walking to the ring without a head guard on for the first time, no vest. The gloves were different as well. Really solid. You can feel the knuckle through the leather. You couldn't do that in the amateurs. I skipped about a bit when I entered the ring, a few shadow-boxing moves while they were announcing the names, Bailey first then mine. The difference in volume when they announced mine was massive. I looked across at Bailey. I thought I was nervous. He was ten times more nervous than me. You could see it in his eyes. He was in shock. It was a big night for him, too. He had never fought in a venue like this. I could see how scared he was. The ring was packed, people everywhere. In the amateurs it is just you and your opponent. I have seen loads of title fights on video, attended world title bouts as well. It never occurred to me to expect that. It just added to the sense of occasion. It was massive.

When the ring started to empty I knew it was time, that the bell would be going any second. I just waited and waited. Like a coiled spring I was. Ready to go. For six weeks I had thought of little else. Now I was just seconds from my professional debut. The referee brought us together, gave his little talk, protect yourself at all times. Good luck. As soon as the bell went Bailey came rushing at me. That was his first mistake. The second he did that everything just came to me automatically. It was like a trigger setting off my boxing responses. I blocked everything else out of my mind, friends, family, crowd. Inside my head there was absolute silence. My jab flicked out. I kept jabbing and jabbing. My feet were moving great. I took the centre of the ring and just waited for him to charge again. As he rushed in I chinned him. I threw a left hook. It skimmed him. Then I caught him with the right and he went over. That was all in the first fifteen seconds. My confidence went up by miles. It showed me that I had the power to knock someone out. I went back to the neutral corner. I knew he was hurt. It was all over his face. I kept the pressure on and within a minute he was over again. His corner threw the towel in. In the amateurs that signals the end of the fight. In the pros it is up to the ref to stop the fight. My immediate response was to walk back to the corner but the ref said box on. He picked the towel up and put it over his shoulder. I was confused. What's going on here? I thought. It didn't last much longer. The ref stopped it after 109 seconds. It was a huge relief.

The pressure that had been building on my shoulders as the youngest Olympic medallist making his pro debut was massive. The moment the ref called a halt it lifted. I was in the game. It was the same as the major amateur competitions. As soon as I got through that first fight I knew more or less how far I was going to go in the event. For me that meant winning, or at least getting to the final. At the Olympics I knew after that first fight that I was going to make it to the final. The first fight is always the worst. After that you know what to expect. Now that I had got my debut out of the way I felt chilled. Everything came easily after that.

In my next fight against Baz Carey I was taken the distance. Oliver still goes on about that now. He can't believe Carey's corner did not pull him out. It was clear he was taking a lot of punishment. He was too brave for his own good. His corner should have intervened.

I wasn't really tested at all until my seventh fight against Laszlo Komjathi in Belfast. It was my first six-rounder. Komjathi had at least six weeks' notice. He had trained properly for the fight. He was tough. He'd been a pro for ten years, fought for a European title. I had trained really hard and was looking forward to measuring my improvement. It was a year almost to the day since I'd fought my last amateur bout against Kindelan. I felt really strong. The training with Oliver had gone well. The fact that I was able to do the six rounds without any trouble showed that. I reckon that the Amir Khan who faced Komjathi would have knocked out the Amir Khan who fought Bailey. That is how much I had come on in ten months.

Once again the crowd were brilliant. The King's Hall is a fantastic, historic venue. Barry McGuigan, who enjoyed some of his best nights there, said the cheer that I got was almost as big as the one reserved for him. It has been the same wherever I have fought, Cardiff, London, Glasgow, Nottingham, the venues have all been packed out. That means so much to me. To know that people have paid good money to come out and watch me live makes me feel very proud.

It is not just those who come to watch the fights. I usually fly in a couple of days before. There is always a press conference on Thursday followed by the weigh-in on Friday. By then the work is done. I might arrange to go to a local gym to stay loose. Apart from that the hardest part is killing time before the fight. That means maybe a walkabout in the city, a meal in a restaurant. People always recognise me. They want to approach me but don't always know how to react. After a while someone will pluck up the courage to ask for a picture or an autograph. It's cool.

Not everybody in Belfast was on the case. A local radio reporter arrived at the Europa Hotel twenty minutes late. All the media stuff was finished. She was lucky I was in the main lobby about to go up to my room to chill. Oliver has my days mapped out. He always includes lots of chill time as the fight approaches. She rushed in and spoke to Asif. I felt sorry for her. She was all over the place, out of breath and looking a bit dishevelled. Asif came over. Amir, have you got time to do one more interview for the local radio? Sure. No problem. I was sat with Oliver and Jed on a couple of sofas arranged around a coffee table. Very cosy. She didn't have a clue who was who. Jed jumped up. Amir, he said, talking to Oliver. This lady has come to interview you. Before Oliver could say anything the microphone was under his nose. So, Amir, how do you like Belfast? I was on the next sofa cracking up. Oliver kept it going for a couple of minutes before putting her out of her misery. I've never seen anyone as embarrassed. It was a nice moment. Much more fun than the normal media stuff.

By then press conferences had become totally routine. The same people asking similar questions. The worst of it is everybody wants to speak to you one-to-one. Each reporter or journalist wants a story to themselves. But they always ask pretty much the same questions. So the next day all the stories are the same anyway. Not that I read them. My dad points out stuff if he likes it. After a few lines I usually give up. If there is anything in them I need to know he tells me.

7

I'm a Celebrity Get Me Out of Here

It did not take long to realise that my success at the Olympics was turning into an industry all of its own. I wasn't just Amir Khan any more, I was Amir Khan, Olympic silver medallist. It was like there were two mes. The real me, and the other one, the commodity, the person who people thought I was. People wanted the commodity to fulfil all sorts of requests, attend the opening of functions, charity events. I would be at one do and someone would come up to me and ask me to help out with this project, that project. They would go into great detail about what they wanted me to do. I would glaze over. Every day was mad. I had no idea what I was doing from one moment to the next, yet people would be trying to make all these arrangements with me. To them no one else had thought of the idea. The fact was everybody had the same idea. And they all wanted me.

Stuff like that takes a lot out of you. People don't realise. At every event there is always one who likes to offer advice. I have met some of the most knowledgeable boxing coaches in the world at some of the dos I have been to since the Olympics. They tell me how to throw a left hook, how to cover up, how to punch. I know that the only time most of them have had a fight is in the street. They have not got a clue. I've had some people ask why I haven't fought Mike Tyson. I've had others challenge me to charity fights. All of them serious.

My focus is on the boxing. That is hard enough. If I were to oblige everybody when they wanted me to do stuff I would never have time to train. My career would be over. I never like to disappoint anybody. I will always try to help when I can. But it was getting silly. We needed to get organised. We had to get professional about things, because the people who were approaching us were very professional in going about what they wanted. Dad was running around like a headless chicken trying to organise everything.

We set up an office in St George's Road in Bolton. My uncle Taz, my sister Tabinda and my business manager Asif run it. It made sense for my family to do it. I feel comfortable with them involved. We could have gone out and signed with a big sports agency to look after everything. But that's not us. We have a commercial association with SFX. Nothing too big. At the office there is enough work to keep an army busy. We might have to get more people in. A lot of it is dealing with charity requests, mail, that sort of thing. I get mail addressed just to Amir Khan, Bolton. It always finds me. We try to balance things between commercial activity and charitable stuff. I go to hospitals, turn on lights at Christmas, hand over cheques, that sort of thing. On the commercial side more stuff has probably been turned down than we have accepted. An agreement has been made with Reebok. That was great. I get to wear some cool gear. Moschino help me out with stuff as well. As a 'celebrity' people always want to give you things. I get so much stuff that my mates come round to the house to choose what they want. I make sure they get the old stuff, though. That is not the main thing for us. The office operates to make my life run smoothly. Without it nothing would work. It is not all glamour either. It is mostly formal stuff. And mostly the events I attend involve a lot of time listening to people a lot older than me. Whenever I go to big functions I always take a mate with me.

There have been some fantastic things as well. While we were still out in Athens I was invited to take part in a special edition of *Superstars* in Spain. I was chuffed to be included in an all-star cast of famous sportsmen, people who I had only ever seen on TV. It coincided with Bolton's first match at the Reebok after we got back from the Olympics. And not just any old match. It was against Manchester United. Bolton wanted me to do a lap of honour before the game. I was living a dream. I wanted to do everything. So I flew to Spain on the Thursday before the match, did a couple of *Superstars* events that night and on Friday. On Saturday morning I was flown back to Manchester in a private jet and taken to the Reebok with a police escort. It was hard to take it all in. I felt like a Hollywood superstar. I arrived half an hour before the kick-off and went straight in to see the manager Sam Allardyce, big Sam to everybody in Bolton. He was brilliant. He took me into his office and gave me a big hug. He wanted to know everything about the Olympics, how it went. What the Olympic final against Kindelan was like. I looked at the clock. It was 2.35 p.m., twenty-five minutes before kick-off. I asked him about the team, who was playing. Never mind about that, he said, I want to hear about you.

About quarter to three he handed me a team-sheet and took me down to the changing room. He said, I want you to go in there and tell that lot what you have achieved, a seventeen-year-old lad winning silver at the Olympics. Go in there and gee them up. I didn't have a clue what I was going to say. We walked in and Sam said, listen, I want you to meet our most famous supporter. He's flown all the way from Spain this morning just to see you. The players all clapped and cheered. Sam said, Amir is going to say a few words. There I was, a seventeen-year-old kid, stuck in front of players like Jay-Jay Okocha, Kevin Nolan and Stelios. In a squeaky, teenage voice I blurted out the first thing that came into my head: don't let the Mancs beat you! The bell went to signal it was time to go out. I walked out of the changing room and there, right in front of me, all lined up, was the whole United team led by Roy Keane. It was amazing. Ryan Giggs, Paul Scholes, Cristiano Ronaldo, Rio Ferdinand, all standing there ready to go on the pitch. Keane spotted me. He came up. Amir, well done in the Olympics. You did really well. I love my boxing. You did the country proud. My face lit up. Cheers, mate, I said. I couldn't think of anything else to say. I was starstruck. Then Giggs came over and shook my hand. Even Sir Alex Ferguson shook hands. Come to see us any time, he said.

I did, as well. I took the 2012 flag to United's training ground at Carrington as part of the successful Olympic bid effort. Sir Alex and Keane both signed it. I was shown all around the complex. Another fantastic day.

Back at the Reebok, just before the teams went out, the ref, Matt Messias, came over and said, don't disappear afterwards, I need you to sign an autograph. It was a couple of minutes before kick-off and I'm holding court in the tunnel. Unbelievable.

I was eventually dragged away to do my lap of honour. The noise was massive. I had a shirt made up specially, half Bolton, half United. Bolton would not let me wear it. I had to wear the Wanderers shirt. Fair enough I suppose. The atmosphere was electric. It always is when United are in town. This was even more special. Both sets of fans were cheering and clapping. Normally they are screaming and booing each other. Soon as I left the pitch they were. Up in the stands I was pictured on the big screen cheering when Bolton scored. It was plastered all over *Match of the Day* later. I had to leave ten minutes from the end to return to Spain for the Superstars. Bolton were winning when I left. On the way to the airport I heard on the radio that Alan Smith had equalised in the last minute for United. Honours even. A great day.

The Laureus Awards in Portugal were brilliant. There were loads of famous sportsmen there. We had to put our signatures on this massive wall. I was just walking away after signing my name when David Beckham called me over. I had to do a double take. Is he talking to me? Hey, Amir, I'm a big fan of yours. It turns out he likes boxing and watched all my fights in Athens. He was saying how much he had enjoyed it. He was a really nice lad. It was mad being on first-name terms with David Beckham.

The following day the organisers took us to a race track. Mika Hakkinen, two-times Formula One world champion, was taking people out. And there were some instructors helping. We were all in fireproof suits, proper racing gear. The cars were all sports cars, powerful motors, the Mercedes CLR, the AMG, stuff like that. The people running it asked us to sign a form and put down driving licence numbers. I didn't have a licence. I had only just started having lessons at the time. I was desperate to have a go. I filled in the form but then left the licence bit blank. No one said anything. They obviously never look at these things. I was in the queue with all these stars, Boris Becker, Barry McGuigan, Kelly Holmes. Kelly's manager turned to my mum as I was getting in the car and asked if I had my licence, as a joke. They both laughed. I got in the car, put my foot down and hammered it through the cones. The instructor was having kittens. I burned some serious rubber that day. Loved it. I reckon I was the best driver there.

Being famous is weird. All sorts of people who I have seen on TV but don't really know come up to me at various events to say hello. Craig David pulled up alongside me in his Range Rover in Manchester once. I was driving my Range Rover. Hey, Amir, how are you, man? Good to see you. That sort of stuff. Another time I was walking down the street in Manchester when two lads walked past me on the other side. They were getting really excited, shouting, it's Amir Khan. I was with a mate, Saj. I thought they might have been off a soap or something. They turned out to play for Manchester City. Saj was hopping about. He knows his footballers.

I met Mike Tyson, once at the Midland Hotel in Manchester and another time at a cage-fighting event. He knew all about me.

He knows everything about boxing. He gave me some good advice. I was sitting with Saj. Tyson was telling me about the importance of family, and to be wary of people who claim to be friends but aren't. Saj was getting really excited about people taking photographs of us. Tyson looked at him and said, yeah, guys like that. If you lose everything tomorrow, they'll be gone. Look at him, he said, he's more into the cameras than you are. Saj didn't know where to put himself. Whacking Tyson was not an option. It was amazing meeting him. I've seen all the videos, watched all his fights. And here he was talking to me.

I'm all right with boxers. I recognise them. Beckham, too. He was easy to spot. With stars from other sports it is not so easy. I've never really been into any sport other than boxing. I was invited to take part in a charity football match in aid of the tsunami victims. I was in a celebrity team against Liverpool legends. There were quite a few lads from the soaps, *Coronation Street*, *Hollyoaks*. We were having breakfast in the hotel in Liverpool, my dad, me, Asif, my mate Saj. Danny Jones from McFly came in. Danny is a Bolton lad. He used to play football at the Lads Club. He told everybody I was brilliant at football. Thanks, mate. That's all I needed. Kenny Dalglish, John Barnes, Ian Rush, Kevin Keegan, all there great Liverpool state were there. I was starstruck. Saj was tapping my arm every two minutes, look, it's so and so.

I was starting to get really nervous by the time we arrived at Anfield. They gave us new kit and boots. Barnes and Rush were arguing over the no. 9 shirt. It was hilarious. Helped break the tension. Just before the start Ralph Little received a note from Razor Ruddock saying he would break his legs if he went anywhere near him. Then I got one. It read: To Amir, I won't come near you in case you knock me out. We all fell about.

I thought there would be about 5,000 people in the stadium. It was packed to the rafters: 51,000. We agreed I'd do twenty minutes. They put me on at the same time as Danny. A double substitution. I was on the left wing, Danny on the right. Danny got an early touch. It wasn't his best. He tried to do this fancy trick, tripped over his own feet and headed the ball out as he fell. Everyone laughed. I managed to go eighteen minutes without seeing the ball. I skilfully put myself where the ball wasn't. Then I got my first and only touch. Bang in front of the Kop. I didn't have time to think. The ball came to me. I just swung my foot. Unbelievably I made a decent connection. The ball flew just over the bar. A massive cheer from the Kop. I couldn't have asked for more. When I came off I did an interview. Ripped Danny. It was brilliant.

After the match I was sat next to this bloke. He was talking to me about cricket, about my cousin Saj at Lancashire. I did not have a clue who he was or what he did. So, I said, how are you doing in your sport? It worked. He started talking about cricket again and England. I worked out he was a cricketer, but I still didn't know who he was. It turned out to be Michael Vaughan, the England captain. If I had known that I would have asked him why Saj wasn't in the team more.

I did that on Sky TV once. It was at Old Trafford. I had been invited to a Twenty20 cricket match, Lancashire versus Yorkshire. I was being interviewed. They asked me what I thought about the game. I said Lancashire had got it wrong because Saj Mahmood wasn't playing. My cousin and Andrew Flintoff were the only cricket players I knew. There was another guy stood at the side of me. The interviewer pointed to him and said, there's the manager, ask him. So I turned to him and said, what's happening, man, why's he not playing? He laughed. We'll have a chat later, he said. It was Mike Watkinson, Lancashire's cricket manager. We never had that chat.

Saj is twenty-four now, coming to his peak. He needs to be playing. I want him to go right to the top, to represent England regularly. He has spent a lot of time around the fringe. They seem funny in cricket. It's as if you can't be any good if you are young. All I know is that Saj has always been brilliant with a bat or a ball in his hand. It would be great for the family if he was picked for Lancashire and England regularly, two cousins representing their country at elite level.

Sometimes I like to surprise people. At an airport I noticed this little kid staring at me. I could see that he was too shy to come up. So I walked over to him, said hi, how ya doin'? The smile on his face and on his parents' faces was worth any amount of money. Sometimes it's nice to be able to do something like that, to show people that I'm just like them, a normal lad. My life might not be normal any more compared to others', but I'm the same lad I've always been. I'm not a celebrity at home, I tell you. My mum still has my number. If my room isn't tidy she goes mad at me. What's all this? Clothes all over the place. Tidy it up. I do as well.

I've got used to the celebrity bit now. You learn how to deal with it. Though I still get freaked when I see my face staring down at me from billboards in the street, stuff like that. People see my picture on the board then notice me walking past. They start tapping each other. It's funny. Once I was watching *Coronation Street*. One of the characters said to the other, oi, who do you think you are, Amir Khan? Brilliant that was, I liked that.

Sometimes it is just as embarrassing when people don't recognise you. On a flight to Pakistan, a couple of kids found out that I was on the plane and kept running up to my seat. I was sat in business class. The stewardess had no idea who I was and was telling people to get out. This is business class, you can't come in here. Back to your seats. She took them back to their parents and asked why they kept going into business asking for my autograph. They told her. She felt bad. We had a laugh about it after.

On another trip to the Bahamas someone asked me if I was a footballer for Manchester United. I don't know who they thought I was. Yes, I said. I play for United. I feel bad about that now because there is someone wandering around the Bahamas telling people they met a famous United player. As far as I know there aren't many Asian kids in football, let alone at United.

The Bahamas trip was one of the best things I've done. A brilliant experience. I was invited on a Virgin Airways trip to Cuba and the Bahamas to celebrate Virgin's first flight there. Sir Richard Branson knew about Cuba and boxing, and about my fight with Mario Kindelan. He put two and two together and invited me along as part of the PR activity. Everybody knew me there. I was with Sir Richard Branson, this famous businessman, one of the richest men in the world, but all the Cubans seemed more interested in me. It was very embarrassing. They are mad about their boxing.

We were only there for a day. We were supposed to go on a sightseeing tour with Richard visiting a factory that makes cigars. A request came through from the Cuban sports minister saying he would like to meet Amir Khan, could I go to the sports ministry? Sir Richard's assistant Paul explained that I was with Sir Richard and that it would not be possible, terribly sorry. They said, no, no, you don't understand, the Cuban sports minister would like to see you. In Cuba the sports minister is a big man, massively important. Richard was great. He said, yeah, let's go, I'll come with you.

We had a police escort all the way. When we got there we were all sat around this table, myself, my manager Asif, my dad, uncle, Sir Richard and his PA, Paul. The room was full of photos of Cuba's boxing greats, Teofilo Stevenson, Felix Savon, Mario Kindelan. The minister was speaking to me constantly. I was saying things like, I'm here as a guest of Sir Richard Branson, pointing to Richard to try to involve him in the conversation. He took no notice and kept talking to me. He seemed mesmerised. You beat our legend after the Olympics, our no. 1 boxer. I had another go. I love Cuban sport, but if it were not for Sir Richard, etc. The result was exactly the same. The man who was investing millions trying to open up Cuba to a new market was being completely ignored. Richard was fine about it. He just laughed. He's a good bloke. Really down to earth.

After that we went for a meal at a restaurant. The owner came up to the table. He said to me, are you the boxer from England, Amir Khan? I said yes. Just wait there, he said. He came back with a big scrapbook. In it was a picture of Muhammad Ali having a meal. He asked if he could have a picture of me to go in the book. Fine, I said. We'll do it after we have eaten the food. Great, he said. When we had finished eating he came back with a proper photographer and lighting equipment. It was like posing for a magazine shoot. He did a big number on me.

It was not long after I had beaten Kindelan in my last amateur fight. We were taken to see the Cuban training camp. I'd never been there before. Everybody was just looking at me. It was like a hostel. As we walked across a courtyard to the gym you could see heads popping up at the windows. They were all whispering my name. Khan, Khan, it's Khan. It was amazing. Stevenson, Savon, Kindelan were all there. Stevenson, this Cuban heavyweight legend, came up to me. He wanted my autograph. I couldn't believe it. It was awesome. Cuba is like the Brazil of amateur boxing. When you are growing up, learning about boxing, all you hear about is Cuban fighters. At major tournaments you always look out for the Cubans. There is massive mystique about them. And here I was surrounded by legends like Stevenson and Savon. And they wanted my autograph. I took photographs with them. Mega.

Looking at that facility it is obvious how the Cubans turn out great fighters. First of all the old stars come back and help with the coaching. Can you imagine having Stevenson and Savon showing you the ropes? It is almost as good as being taught to fight by Muhammad Ali and Sugar Ray Leonard. No wonder Kindelan turned out to be so good. Secondly the system is run like a professional training camp. There is no need to give the boxers grants. Everything is funded by the state. That would never happen here.

The Cuba trip was a massive jolly. It's not all take, though. I try to give a lot back when I can. Obviously I've been to Pakistan twice to help raise awareness of the earthquake disaster. People are always looking to use celebrities to push good causes. If I have time I help out. A month after I came back from Pakistan I played in a charity football tournament at Bradford City for Sharon Beshenivsky, the police officer murdered by two Asians during a robbery. As a family we have lots of connections in Bradford. I just wanted to do what I could. And football is not my thing. Once when a TV crew came to video me playing football at Bolton College I only lasted five minutes. I fell over twice and ended up in goal.

I wasn't much better in Bradford. When I turned up they couldn't find a parking space for me. I didn't mind that so much, but the moment I stop my car at public events these days it disappears underneath a mass of people. It was mobbed. I managed to get into the stadium through a side door then ended up in the wrong dressing room full of blokes off *Coronation Street*. Both teams were packed with celebrities. I think it was Mike Baldwin's son who said, hey, Amir, come and play for us. Lucky for them I didn't. At least I lasted longer than Paul Jewell, the Wigan manager. There is a lot of local rivalry between Wigan and Bolton in the Premiership. Paul limped off after about five minutes clutching his groin. I tried not to laugh. I started on the bench. I was coming up to my fight in Belfast against Komjathi. Taz told the organisers that I could only play twenty minutes max. They had to bring me on early because of the kids climbing on to the dugout for autographs. They thought the dugout might collapse.

It was a bit embarrassing in the warm-up. I just ran around a lot trying to avoid the ball. Football is a completely different rhythm to boxing. I can run around all day but when that ball comes anywhere near me, and I try to kick it, I lose coordination. One level of the main stand was packed. I didn't want to look rubbish in front of loads of people. The other lads could all play a bit. Paul Jewell was a pro. And they weren't pulling out of the tackles. My uncle was stood at the side of the dugout cringing. When I came on I got into it. I didn't have a clue what I was doing. I just followed the ball. The next thing I know the ball comes across and I'm in front of goal with only the goalkeeper to beat. I swung my boot. I got a good connection. The ball flew in. One–nil to the whites. I came off before half-time. I was happy to be in one piece.

Afterwards we celebrated in Mumtaz, a curry house in Great Horton Road, Bradford. It's one of my favourite restaurants. Saj was ripping me about my football. He reckons he can play a bit. So what? He'll never score a goal like mine at Bradford.

Two weeks later I made my debut at the King's Hall in Belfast against Komjathi, my seventh fight as a pro. I took a bit of stick for showboating. The press guys got a bit excited about me standing in the corner with my hands by my sides. I was never in any trouble. I was pleased with my performance. Pleased to be back in the ring. Pleased to do six rounds for the first time in my career. I could have gone another six, no problem. One day I will have to. One day I'll be world champion.

A couple of weeks after the Belfast fight I was back in Bradford for a party in the park, a big summer do. The organisers asked if I would put in an appearance for a couple of hours in the afternoon. Not a problem. Over we went, me and Taz. They put me in a tent. The idea was that I would sign autographs and pose for pictures from two in the afternoon until four. I did a few interviews for Asian TV and radio. They were asking me about the day, what I thought about it. I couldn't get out of the tent to walk about but it was obvious that everybody was having a brilliant time. It wasn't just Asian people there. All communities were represented. No barriers. At five o'clock I was still there. It had been raining hard for about forty minutes but the queues were still stacked up outside. They had to sneak me out of a back entrance in the end. I didn't like doing it but we had another do that evening. Taz went to the front to tell people that I had left the tent, to apologise on my behalf for having to leave and to explain that there was no point hanging around.

They didn't believe him. When he came back to the car you could see hundreds of people still gathered around that tent waiting for a glimpse of me. We talked about it on the way back to Bolton. People were telling me how their kids had stayed up late to watch the fight in Belfast. Old boys were congratulating me for the good job I was doing for the Asian community. It was a reminder of how important I had become for these people. Days like that make me feel important in a positive way and spur me on to work even harder.

The day before, I paid my first visit to a jail, Ranby, a category C prison in Nottingham. I was in between fights, the best time for me to do stuff like that. The inmates had started a charity fund and wanted me to open it officially. The governor sent an email. It would only take forty minutes. We were going to a charity dinner in Nottingham that night anyway so it wasn't a problem to go there first. You hear all sorts of stuff about prisons. I was interested to see what it would be like.

Mick, Saj, Taz and my dad all came, too. We were only visiting the part of the prison where they kept the gym. I didn't see any cells. Once inside you go through one door then they bolt it shut before opening another for security reasons. The first thing I noticed was the size of the guys in there. They were massive. Even the older blokes. I wouldn't have got in the ring with any of them. They were a bit standoffish at first. They were all training. Most of the guys were coming to the end of their time. I was introduced to a couple then everybody started to relax. I was basically talking to them about boxing and fitness.

There was a punchbag in the corner. They wanted to know if they were hitting the bag correctly. One guy put the gloves on and started punching away like mad. He was like me in my early amateur fights. Don't forget to breathe, I said. He fell about laughing. They all said that I looked bigger on TV. I never thought that I would be a hero to guys like them. You never think that people in prisons would be watching your fights. They loved their boxing. They could have chosen anybody to open the fund for them, but they chose me. Afterwards we went back to the governor's office for the official ceremony. It was another new experience for me.

In the evening a glove and a signed picture raised more than £6,000 at a charity do organised by the Midlands Doctors Association. The money was going towards the building of a hospital in Muzaffarabad in the Pakistan earthquake zone. That's one of the good things about being famous. You can make a difference.

8

Keeping It in the Family

Every member of my family has helped in his or her own way. I couldn't have done it without them. But three people in particular travelled nearly every inch of the way, from my first amateur fight in Stoke to the Olympic Games in Athens. They are as big a part of the Amir Khan story as I am.

Shahid, my uncle Terry

My uncle Terry, Saj Mahmood's dad, was the young pioneer of the family. He came over to Bolton when my grandad had sorted out a place to live. It was 1967. He was just ten years old. He did not speak a word of English. He was the first member of the family to taste the better life that Grandad was planning for the Khans. It didn't feel better when he landed at the airport. It was July. The weather in Pakistan was hot. He did not want to come. He was leaving his brother and sisters behind, my dad included. He was told about the different language and the colder weather. At ten, it did not seem like that good a deal. He was the guinea pig. Gran told him that he must settle and do well at school so that everybody else could follow him out.

Education was the big thing for my grandparents. My

grandad had travelled in the army. He had seen that village life in rural Pakistan did not offer his children much opportunity in a world that was changing rapidly. There are 150 million people in Pakistan. Education, especially in rural places, is not top of the government's list of priorities. Schooling is pretty basic. Grandad wanted something better for his children, he wanted his kids to be educated in England. In Pakistan only important people spoke English. Grandad worked it out that if his kids had any chance of being important people in some way they must first speak English. Uncle Terry arrived at Heathrow airport on the last day of July clinging to the idea that the rest of the family would be following soon. It took almost four years for that to happen. He travelled up to Bolton in a Transit van that Grandad had organised. Grandad was living in Orm Street then, sharing a house with three others who had come over from Pakistan and Bangladesh like him to make their fortune.

Terry was the only child in the house. He arrived in time to start the school year at Gaskell Street Primary School. There were not many Asians there. He had to learn quickly. He had no choice. The whole family has heard the story of his first break time. He was stood in the doorway leading out to the playground. Two girls came over to him. They were speaking to him but he had no idea what they were trying to say. He raised his hand to acknowledge them as if to say, yes, I'm coming, then he ran off through the crowds of kids rushing into the yard. It was too much for him. The girls were just being friendly. But Terry wasn't quite ready for friends. Instinct told him to run for it to spare his embarrassment. It was tough. Running away from situations was the only way he could cope.

Grandad was working twelve-hour shifts in the mill from six in the morning until six at night. Every day he would leave a flask of tea for when Terry came home from school in the afternoon. By the time he moved to secondary school, Terry was getting the hang of things. Grandad used to give him two new words to learn a day and two shillings to spend. That is 10p in today's money. One shilling had twelve pennies in it. Fish, chips and peas cost him ninepence. That left the rest for sweets. My uncle went to Whitecroft School. There are houses now where the school used to be. Another example of how much things have changed in Bolton. He was the only Asian boy in his class.

As more families came over Terry was given the job of teaching the new kids English at the school. By the time my dad arrived with my two aunties in 1970 Grandad had bought a house on Church Street and Terry was on his way. He did OK at school, well enough to be offered a job as an apprentice engineer at British Aerospace. The family was very proud. To get an apprenticeship at a firm like British Aerospace was a big thing. Terry thought he had a job for life. And it was there that the seeds of my cousin Saj's international cricket career were sewn. Terry used to play a bit at school but did not take it that seriously until he started his apprenticeship. British Aerospace had a cricket team that played in the Bolton Association. That was proper cricket. In Pakistan cricket is everything, the only sport that really matters. Cricket has always been a big thing in Lancashire, too. Opener Mudassar Nazar and the great Javed Miandad, who both played Test cricket for Pakistan, played in the Bolton Association. You had to be a decent player to get a game. Terry was a swing bowler, medium quick. He says he was like Ian Botham, swinging it a mile. He reckons he clean bowled Anwar Khan, who played one Test match for Pakistan, in a career-best spell of 9 for 19. I'd love to get hold of that scorecard.

Terry eventually qualified as an engineer but he was made redundant. It was 1981. Places were shutting down all over Bolton. He found a job in Slough. He agreed a price on a house, £32,000. While he was waiting for the mortgage to come through the guy sold it to a cash buyer. Saj had come along by this time and was staying in Bolton with his mum. The plan was to move south when Terry had sorted out a house. Terry was coming back to Bolton every weekend. When the house fell through he asked Gran to speak to Grandad about coming back up north permanently. He didn't want to make the call himself. He didn't want to seem like a failure in front of his dad. Gran smoothed it over for him to come home otherwise Saj would have ended up being a southerner and playing cricket for Middlesex.

Terry took a job as a taxi driver. He could have signed on while he waited for an engineering job to turn up but he was too proud to go on the dole. He wanted more than just survival. He was turned down by the police because he was too short, half an inch below the height restriction. He was 5ft 8ins. It is funny to see him stood next to Saj now. Saj is massive, 6ft 4ins. When he was thirty-five, the police dropped all restrictions. He reapplied and got in. PC Mahmood, another proud day for the Khan family.

In Pakistan when Uncle Terry and my dad were born, family names didn't matter that much. You could choose any name you fancied, like a first name here. That's why I'm a Khan and Saj is a Mahmood, because Lall chose different names for his kids. It's changing now. The authorities in Pakistan are tightening up. They realise that they have to get into step with other parts of the world. In the past it was down to the village elders to keep a record of who was related to whom.

Shajaad, my dad

In 1970 it was my dad Shajaad's turn to make the trip from Pakistan. At least he had Gran and his sisters for company. He doesn't remember too much about his early days in Bolton except that it was always sunny. He must have imagined it. Like Terry Dad did not disgrace himself at school. He tells people he was an average student. His bag was always cars. He wouldn't have seen that many as a kid growing up in Matore. He doesn't care what they look like too much, that's my thing. He prefers looking under the bonnet. He likes engines and getting his hands dirty. When Grandad bought Terry a car my dad was always checking the oil and tyre pressures. Terry never had to clean it once.

At weekends Dad used to help out at a garage on Chorley Old Road. Once again he'd be under the bonnet, changing oil and wheels, jacking the cars up, checking the brakes. In those days car repair was big business. According to my dad people couldn't afford new cars. They had to keep old ones running. It was mad. Dad didn't earn a penny at that garage. It was an investment he said. It paid off. Like Terry, Dad managed to get an apprenticeship, as a mechanic at Kearsley Van Hire. It was a real feather in his cap. There was a lot of competition for jobs in the trades, because you got a wage while you were learning the job. Grandad and Gran were just happy to see their second son follow in the footsteps of the first. As well as a good job, Dad also got a new name.

There were a few lads in for the position. Dad was behind another Asian on the day he went for his interview. He followed him into the office. The boss, a man called Vincent Ingram, asked him loads of questions then at the end he asked him what he thought of dogs. Dad said, what do you mean? Ingram said, do you get on with dogs? They don't bother me, said Dad. Great, Ingram said, you've got the job. He told my dad that he was going to give the job to the other kid but he couldn't because he hated dogs. Ingram had a husky. Dad said it had a great big head like a bear, a good guard dog. So Dad passed the dog test but Ingram couldn't pronounce his name. Do you mind if I call you Shah? Not a problem, said Dad. He's been Shah ever since.

Dad served his time going to day release at college and getting his City and Guilds qualification. When the garage changed hands Dad decided to go it alone, something he had always fancied doing. It was 1983, old Ingram had retired and the new management were banging the drum. Dad didn't go for that. He was just twenty-two. It was a big year for my dad. He got married and Lall passed away in Pakistan. My dad became the main breadwinner in the house. As well as a young wife to support, he had to look after Gran and his younger brother Taz. Before long, Tabinda was on the scene followed by me. We were living in Centre Gardens at the time, just behind Terry's house. Having Terry, who had just moved back up from Slough, close by helped a lot. Family is a massive thing in Pakistan. Relations from different generations often live in the same house. It saves money. About a third of the 150 million population of Pakistan lives below the poverty line. They have no choice but to share a home. Pakistani and Asian families in England are still close, but these days kids tend to move into their own places when they grow up. Usually just around the corner.

Dad got his head down and worked. He'd made a few contacts, done a few foreigners (extra commissions) at weekends, built up a tiny customer base. He rented a small unit in Farnworth for £35 a week. It had room for only one car, but it had a pit. That was the clincher. All the jobs he used to do at night for extra cash he could do during the day now. The business took off. Work was coming in quickly. Soon he had moved to bigger premises in Farnworth. There was space for two cars there. Dad must have known what he was doing. He's a grafter. Never says no to anybody. If anyone needed something doing in those early days, he would stay until the job was finished. That's why people always came back.

He moved on again, setting up a garage in Bolton with a partner, Vinny Mullready. Vinny was a panel beater. He ran the body shop while Dad fixed the cars. When I was six Dad bought a scrapyard. Instead of fixing cars, he broke them. He'd buy write-offs from insurance companies, strip them down into spares and sell the parts on. His speciality was Japanese cars. The parts were not expensive so there was a decent market. The business was good enough for Mum and Dad to move to a bigger house in Tudor Avenue, just off Chorley New Road. When Taz and Tabinda got married they bought houses close to Tudor Avenue, keeping the family nearby.

The beauty of the breakers' yard was that Dad had time to travel with me. By the time I started boxing competitively, the yard was running itself. Dad would leave someone in charge while we went here, there and everywhere with Bury ABC. By the time I got to the Olympics Dad was never there. He was off for weeks at a time travelling to qualifiers with me. He's sold the business now. Secretly I think he misses it.

Tahir, my uncle Taz

Uncle Taz was the baby in the house, the only one of Grandad and Gran's five kids to be born in England. He was also the brains of the family, the only one to go to university. That was the reason Grandad brought everybody to England in the first place, to make sure his children received a proper education. Grandad passed away when Taz was just eleven. Taz did him proud. He is ten years younger than my dad, a different generation really, and like me Bolton born and bred. He was at Smithills at the same time as Ronnie Irani, the year below. He also went to Bolton Community College like me before he went to university. When I came back from the Olympics and Dad set up the office in St George's Road above Asif's taxi place, Taz quit his job to help run the business side of my career with Asif. He's a computer whiz kid. He soon had all the technical stuff in place. Tabinda makes sure the office runs smoothly. She's brilliant, a terrific organiser.

It was a massive thing when Taz went to university. A big step. He did electronics at Bolton College then went to the University of Hertfordshire in Hatfield to do a degree in electronic and electrical engineering. Gran did not want him to go all that way. Taz wanted to be independent. She finally relented then tried to get him to stay with a relative who lives near the college. He refused. He wanted to live in the halls of residence with the rest of the students. In his second year he rented a place with some mates. My dad wanted to buy a house for him so that he could rent it with his mates. He was still on his independent thing and didn't take up the offer. He wishes he had now. Being out on his own didn't stop Taz coming home at weekends with his washing and raiding the cupboards for food.

He graduated from there in 1994. Everyone was massively proud, buzzing. I have a similar relationship with Taz as he had with my dad and Terry. Though they are brothers he was much younger than them. They used to look out for him. Now he is looking out for me. He takes his responsibilities too seriously at times. Scares my mates. When we went on holiday to Dubai after the Olympics we had to pretend to go back to our rooms at night then sneak out when he had gone to bed. He still phones me to check where I am.

When he finished uni he worked at Dad's yard until he got a job. Gran made him go. She didn't want Taz hanging around doing nothing while he was applying for jobs. She didn't really understand the rules. She was pleased that Taz had got a degree but she thought he should be in work straight away. She thought Taz had it easy being at home all day. She didn't realise it sometimes took time to get interviews and stuff. She wanted him to help his brothers. He loved it. It opened his eyes to what happened in the workplace. And he got a lift to work every day.

His first proper job was at an IT firm in Rawtenstall. He was an account manager. Dead cool. I cost him most of his wages in computer games. It was costing him so much that he had to put a chip in the games console to make them compatible with games brought in cheaper from abroad. His degree wasn't wasted. Taz was quite a high flyer by the time I got to the Olympics. It's great that he came over to work alongside my dad and Asif to help run my career. It's important to me that my family are involved. I can concentrate on the fighting while Dad and Taz get on with all the other stuff. Taz basically runs my diary, goes to meetings and sets things up.

All I know when I get up in the morning is that I have to be at the gym by 10 a.m. That's enough for me to worry about. I couldn't manage if I had other stuff to worry about as well. Taz tells me where I need to be, at what time, and I turn up. Sometimes when I've had a heavy session in the gym I feel like sleeping in the afternoon. But if there is something in the diary I always go. I hate letting people down. Once, after the Olympics, Mick had promised an amateur club in Grange-over-Sands that I would attend a dinner. The bloke who ran it was a mate of Mick's. It was on a Friday night. The last place I fancied going was Grange-over-Sands. No disrespect to the club, or the town, but it is not a place I will go back to in a hurry. I'm glad I went though. I got a great reception.

Cousin Saj, a boyhood hero

Terry helped set up a cricket team for Asian players called West Bolton. That's where super Saj learned his trade. Every time the team was short Saj used to step in. By eleven he was showing real potential. A friend of Terry's was involved with the Bolton Indian cricket club. He suggested Saj play there in the junior team. After about three weeks the club had to pull him out of the side because he was too good. Saj was the family superstar at that time. He was a real hero to me. Terry had to move him on to

Astley Bridge, a much bigger club in north Bolton. He was scoring loads of runs and taking stacks of wickets. From there he went on to represent the league side. He was leading run-scorer and wicket-taker for them. If he didn't get man of the match after every game there was an inquest at home.

Every year Terry took Saj for trials at Lancashire. They kept saying, no, we'll have a look next year. Then when he was seventeen, he got a call from Lancashire to fill in for a bowler who was injured. He was top wicket-taker and run-scorer. He was asked to stand in for a second time. The result was the same. He ended up playing a full season for the Lancashire U-17s. Jimmy Anderson was in the same team, but Saj was the star man. He ended up with twenty-one wickets, more than any other bowler, and with a batting average of 49. He started out batting at ten. The next best average was about 30.

Around that time I had my first amateur fight in Stoke-on-Trent. Terry and Saj were there with Dad and Taz. Terry gave me a fiver when I won. He wanted to give me a tenner, but he only had a fiver in his pocket. Terry was so chuffed at my performance. Taz used to buy me video games. I had to win three bouts on the trot to get a new game. I've still got them in my room. My younger cousins play with them now.

Saj never looked back after that season. Lancashire eventually offered him a scholarship. It was a massive thing for the family when that happened. We were all buzzing off it. He made his first-team debut against Hampshire in August 2002. He only got two overs in because of rain. At the end of 2003 when I was pushing the ABA to go to the Olympic qualifiers Saj was picked to tour with the England Academy side in India. Everything seemed to be going for us at the same time. Saj is like me, he loves playing and competing at his sport, but he is not big on history. He knows the names but not the faces. After one of the games in India he was approached by a guy who ran a cricket academy there. Saj had played well and the guy wanted him to bowl in the academy nets. He said to Saj, do you know who I am? No, said Saj. It was only Dennis Lillee, one of the best bowlers that ever lived. Saj had heard of him but didn't have a clue what he looked like. The next day Saj went for a net session. Lillee raved about him. After I had qualified for the Olympics Saj was called into the England one-day squad and made his debut against New Zealand. Another proud day for the family. My other cousin, Saj's younger brother Rakeb, is good enough to make it, too. He's a year younger than me. He plays for Astley Bridge. Lancashire are looking at him. Saj, Rakeb, me and my younger brother Harry have all had the family behind us. Without them none of us would have progressed this far. They have made massive sacrifices. It's harder for Harry and Rakeb because their older brothers have done well. They will always be measured against us. But they are in there giving it a go. It's what we do.

9

Fighting Back the Tears

I was in training for my third fight against Steve Gethin when the news broke. There had been a massive earthquake in Pakistan, not far from our family home in the north of the country. Usually these kinds of events don't touch you. You watch disasters on TV and it seems so far away. This was different. It affected lots of people I knew. It seemed that every Pakistani family in Bolton knew somebody who had lost friends and family, their homes. My dad phoned Pakistan to make sure everybody was OK. Everybody we knew personally was safe. They said they felt the tremors, nothing more than that.

As the day went on we heard that people were leaving Bolton immediately to go to Pakistan. A brother, sister, cousin, grandparent had died. I was listening to all this going on around me. I was watching news bulletins. Naturally you want to do something to help. I knew that I could. The London bombings were a steep learning curve for me. They threw me into the media spotlight in a way I had not known before. I was a news item not a sports story, the face of Asians in a way. That experience taught me that I could change things a lot. That I could make a difference.

In March 2005 I ran the Wilmslow half-marathon in aid of the tsunami appeal. I raised £107,000. A friend of mine, Nabeel Chowdery, is a property developer. He got businesses, banks and other professional people to back me. That was a massive amount. I was chuffed with that. Before that I had run only short distances, two, three miles, explosive stuff. I did it in one hour forty minutes. I felt such a sense of achievement. At one point it was hurting so much I wasn't sure if I could keep going. It was tough. But then you remember why you are doing it.

As soon as I heard, I wanted to do something for the earthquake victims. I wasn't sure what exactly. We contacted a few charities. At the same time Oxfam got in touch with us through a woman called Shaista Aziz. She was from a Pakistani background, too. That connection swung it really. The earthquake struck about 10 a.m. UK time on 8 October 2005. By 6 p.m. the same day, Shaista was on a plane to Pakistan. She is a brilliant woman. She has been involved in the coordination of loads of relief programmes all over the world.

The earthquake left more than 70,000 people dead and two million homeless. More than two thirds of the buildings had been smashed to bits. Two weeks after the quake happened there were still thousands of desperate, bewildered people wandering around what was left of the area. By then it was beginning to disappear off TV screens. Shaista knew that the situation was getting worse for people not better. The winter was closing in. Temperatures were dropping fast. She needed to keep the issue alive to ensure that aid kept coming in. Oxfam are upfront about the use of high-profile people to raise awareness. Usually they go for white celebrities because they are better known and attract more media interest. Fair enough. But this time it was me that sprung to mind. She remembered me from the Olympics. Being from a Pakistani background herself, she kept tabs on my career. She made contact with my dad. That got the ball rolling. I couldn't do anything immediately. I had the Gethin fight coming up and was pencilled in to fight again a month after that. It would have to be in the run-up to Christmas.

In the meantime I did lots of fundraisers in Bolton. I went to charity dos, visited schools. The kids would pay 50p or £1 to come to school without their uniforms. I would go in and do a talk about the earthquake and later collect cheques and stuff. The mayor of Bolton opened a special charity dedicated to the victims. Nabeel and I paid £10,000 for some steel storm-proof shelters to be erected. Every little helped.

A week after beating Daniel Thorpe in London I was on a plane to Islamabad. I flew out with Dad, Haroon and Nabeel. We stayed in Matore that night then got up the next morning at 5 a.m. for the one-hour journey back to the airport to meet Shaista. The road there from Islamabad goes through beautiful countryside. You can see the mountains from the city. I used to stare at them as a kid and wonder what it might be like up there. We never went. It was too remote, too inaccessible. There was no such thing as a sightseeing trip. Unless you had to be up there, you wouldn't go.

It was heartbreaking to see it like this. As we got closer to Muzaffarabad, the capital of Pakistani-controlled Kashmir, there were hardly any buildings left. Those that were standing had huge cracks in them. For all I knew there could have been people still in them, their bodies buried in the rubble. The roads were torn apart, great big holes in them. Oxfam were trying to arrange a helicopter for us but it wasn't possible. The roads were almost impossible to drive along and very windy with massive rocks lying about everywhere. We were all feeling sick in the car. I wondered what it must have been like before the earthquake. It can't have been easy at the best of times. It was the middle of nowhere. They were mostly farmers working the land, very poor people.

At first rescuers could not get in or out. It took them a month to open the roads to the more remote areas. By the time we got there the authorities had set up camps. They were like tented villages. I remember it being very cold. I was freezing and I had a big winter coat on. Kids were wandering around in thin clothes and T-shirts. There was no warm clothing for them. It made me wonder how many would survive the winter. It was very emotional. I was fighting back tears the whole time. Because the food shortages were massive, people were literally starving to death. I spent a few hours visiting Chatter Class camp just outside Muzaffarabad. I wasn't there long, but it was long enough for me to understand the horror that people had gone through. People looked lost, devastated. They did not have a clue what was going on. There were three temporary shops set up selling basics. Nabeel and I went in and emptied all of them. We bought bread, milk, eggs, anything we could get our hands on that people might eat. We spent about 10,000 rupees in each shop, roughly £300 in total. The shops closed for the day after that because there was nothing left for them to sell. We took the food into the camp and started to distribute milk cartons and rusks. It felt great just to do something. We were quickly surrounded by people, all wanting the food. Then Shaista came running across and told us to stop. We thought we were helping. She pointed out that it was dangerous to do off-the-cuff stuff like that. It could turn nasty, cause problems in the camps with those that didn't get anything. In my heart I was doing my best for them. It was an impulse thing. But in disaster situations like that everything has to be controlled by the aid agencies or the whole thing can fall apart. Another lesson learned.

I was introduced to loads of children in a temporary school. There must have been a couple of hundred between about four and fourteen gathered around, trying to make the most of their lives, pick up the pieces. Listening to what some of the kids had to say was very hard. I was thinking that had the earthquake struck a few miles to the south my own relatives could have been shattered like this. There were brothers and sisters who had lost their parents, their homes, everything. I met one lad who was about nine years old. He stood up and said his name. He told me that both his parents had been killed. He and his two younger brothers were being looked after by his sister. She was only fourteen. To see him and his brothers like that had a massive effect on me. I was tired and feeling sick. At times I did not think I could carry on. But watching how they were responding to the crisis in their lives kept me going. Shaista kept asking me if I was OK. She explained that if I needed to talk things through at any time she was there. It can be traumatic for people seeing disaster situations for the first time. It was normal to react with shock. I kept thinking what it would be like if I were in their place with no home, no family, no hope. These kids were tough. They adjusted really quickly. They had no choice but to get on with it.

Oxfam were brilliant. I learned how the charities and agencies concentrated on different parts of the relief effort. Oxfam had responsibility for water and sanitation projects, making sure that people had clean drinking water and shelter, areas where they could wash their clothes and bathe. These people had lost everything but at least in the camps Oxfam gave them a bit of dignity. That meant a lot to them.

The experience showed me how strong people are when the chips are down. You would never think that people could build their lives back up after something like that. In England we have everything done for us. The government makes sure that people have a certain standard of living. And if there is an emergency of any kind, help is always at hand. Up there in those mountains the people had nothing. In the early stages of the disaster not even any help. Belief got them through. And the huge support of the aid agencies. I felt proud to be doing my bit. We did so much that day. The cameras were with us the whole time, following me around. The people didn't know who I was. But when they were told that I was a boxer who won a medal at the Olympic Games they were very excited. They asked me about my life and about boxing. How did I get into it? How old was I? What was life like in Bolton? In asking those kinds of questions it showed that in their minds they were starting to move away from their own predicament. It was a relief to be talking about my own life in a way. They were thrilled that someone famous had come to help. It showed them that the world cared about their plight, that they were not alone.

I did a lot of interviews for the media. It was hard. I did not really feel like talking about what I had seen. I think I was probably in shock myself. It was very upsetting. When you see little kids in that position it breaks your heart. I was dog-tired at the end. I did all the interviews then we had a three-and-a-half-hour drive back to Islamabad. It was one of the hardest days of my life. I had learned so much and was determined to carry on the fight for the victims when I got back to England. It was far from over for them. They had a bitterly cold winter to get through. Many more would die in the snows before I returned in April. I didn't want their plight to be forgotten.

When we got back to England my dad said I should take a couple of days off. I was tired, but I didn't want to. There was a dinner to attend almost immediately. I was keen to raise some more money. I felt really good doing that. I knew how much it would be needed. I had just turned nineteen, but I felt responsible for keeping the issue alive. I told those kids that I would go back to England to get help. I was determined to do what I could. The response I got was amazing. I was auctioning gloves everywhere. One glove went for £5,000 at an auction in Bradford. A few weeks later at an event in Glasgow another one also went for £5,000. That figure was then matched by a businessman to take it to £10,000. Overall my uncle Taz reckons we have raised more than a quarter of a million pounds for charities including the earthquake victims.

Four months later I made a second trip to the disaster zone. There was still much to be done. Oxfam reckon that 40 per cent of those made homeless, about 800,000 people, face a second winter in camps. Shaista got back in touch. She wanted to take a couple of journalists on the trip from England as well as a film crew from ITN. One of the journalists was from the *Daily*

Mirror, another from the *Sunday Times*. I was cool with that. It was the six-month anniversary of the earthquake. Oxfam wanted it back in the news.

Driving up the long mountain roads to Muzaffarabad, my mind kept going back to the people that I had met in December. It was the women and children that stuck in my mind most. They looked so weak and helpless. By now the weather was really hot. In the summer months the extreme heat is as big a problem as the biting cold in the winter when there is no place to shelter. We arrived at Chatter Class to find that there were no tents. It was just a field. There were a few families there, scattered about. I saw a couple of kids that I spoke to on my first visit. I asked what was happening. They told me that they were being moved on. The authorities had asked them to go back to their homes. They had no idea what they would find. They were probably going home to nothing, a situation that was no better than the camps. Shaista said that Oxfam would try to make sure that when they got home there would at least be fresh water in place. They faced a ten-hour drive plus a two-hour walk to make it home. It was tough listening to their story. I was glad they had made it through the winter and that they had remembered me. But you could see the hurt and desperation in their eyes. It was still going to be hard for them when they got back home.

I came across a lot of brave, tough people. Their stories were sad but inspiring at the same time. It made me thankful for what I had. At another camp there was one woman whose face I'll never forget. She lost her husband in the earthquake. She had four kids. One was blind. They were living in a scruffy tent near Muzaffarabad. The camp was very bad, the stench rising in the heat. It really hit home. She was the same age as my mum. I couldn't imagine my mother looking after four children in conditions like that.

Oxfam had done a brilliant job in that first six months. Things were still bad but better than they were when I first went up there. In all Oxfam provided water and sanitation for 540,000 people. In addition to that they distributed special tents and shelter kits to more than 350,000 people. It was a massive effort. My job was to help raise more money. To alert people to the desperate situation the victims were still in. The winter was over, but heavy rainfall in the spring had caused massive landslides. These secondary effects were almost as dangerous in terms of disease as the earthquake itself. The temperatures were going up fast. The camps that were still running were getting stuffy and hot. Shaista explained that the risk of cholera outbreaks was huge.

Clean water and sanitation was the biggest challenge in the camps. A lot of the tented villages were set up on paddy fields. That was great in one way because the land was flat. But when it started to rain the fields got waterlogged very quickly. That can lead to all sorts of problems and diseases. Fortunately because of the work Oxfam had done, there were no serious outbreaks.

In the villages around Battagram, Oxfam were able to repair a lot of the water supplies. In Muzaffarabad they supported loads of local projects and went into schools to stress the importance of proper waste disposal and the need for personal hygiene. Doing something as simple as washing hands regularly made a huge difference. When the camps were closed there was still plenty to do to make the area safe. Oxfam had to make sure that toilet pits were filled in and water tanks were taken down for use elsewhere.

Taz had not come on the first trip. He could not believe how bad it was. I told him he should have seen it in December. The journey made him sick. I was knackered myself. I was suffering from jet lag. It didn't feel right to moan about it so I kept going. Like the first trip we were at the earthquake site for only one day. But it was a long day driving up rough mountain roads, getting thrown about in the vehicles. It was not like travelling on the motorway, that's for sure.

Afterwards I did a big press conference in Islamabad. There were a lot of media there, which was great for Oxfam. There was a great deal of coverage in Asia and the Gulf region especially. Oxfam were thrilled at the response. I was too. Everyone was thrilled apart from the man from the *Sunday Times*. I don't usually read stuff written about me. I look at the headlines and a couple of lines then get bored. My dad reads stuff and tells me if there is anything I need to know. He told me about the *Sunday Times* article. It was really hurtful and a shock. The guy was so nice. I thought he was a good bloke. He was asking me loads of questions about boxing, about the business side of boxing. I wanted to forget about boxing for a week. I thought he had come to talk to me about Pakistan and the earthquake. I was thinking to myself that he was really wasting my time and Oxfam's time by doing that. There were so many other things to discuss. But because he seemed a nice guy I just got on with it. If people ask me stuff I answer them as honestly as I can.

When we got home and read the piece everything fell into place. Shortly before leaving for the earthquake zone the second time a clothing deal was done with Reebok. I was chuffed with that. I thought it was cool that a big company like that wanted me to be the face of their sports gear, especially with the Reebok connection in Bolton. It was a big thing for me. It made me proud. As part of the deal I have to wear Reebok stuff in photographs. That's what they pay their money for. In Pakistan I was asked to pose for a picture wearing an Oxfam shirt. Because I had just signed with Reebok, my first big commercial deal, I didn't want to let them down. Shaista wasn't bothered. Oxfam were not offended. It didn't stop others in the picture wearing Oxfam stuff. And most importantly of all, it did not make any difference to the message Oxfam were trying to put across. In my mind I was doing right by Reebok and Oxfam.

The *Sunday Times* did not see it that way. At the start of the article it was all about the T-shirt incident. The journalist was trying to suggest that I might be putting the concerns of Reebok before Oxfam, that there was something cynical going on. That really hurt me. It was rubbish. I knew why I was there. I went because I thought I could help. These were my people, my father's people and his father's people. It was not about Reebok. It was about saving lives, about helping Oxfam to help others. That's why I was there. Those kids in the camps did not care what I was wearing. They were just glad I was there. If there was anything cynical going on it was the tone of the article in the *Sunday Times*. He came back to the T-shirt in the story then asked my dad loads of questions about how I was being managed. I thought the piece was about earthquake victims but he seemed more interested in how I was being managed by my family.

Later on his article suggested that I ended an interview with the *Daily Mirror* journalist because she asked me about a traffic incident that I was involved with in Bolton. And then afterwards that she was asked to go back to Islamabad in a different car. She was, but not because of anything that was said in the interview. She asked my dad earlier if she could have twenty minutes with me on the way back. No problem, my dad said, but if you don't mind when it is over can we swap people around so that we can get off to our own hotel in one car without having to ferry people around to different places? It had been a long day. My uncle Taz was feeling sick. Everybody was tired. She was fine with that. We did the interview, she asked me all about the accident in Bolton. I had no problem with it. It was in the local news five minutes after it happened. I had nothing to be ashamed of. There was a pedestrian involved. I waited at the scene, phoned the police and stuff. No problem. Her report when it came out was brilliant. It seemed that the *Sunday Times* journalist had his own agenda.

It was the first negative story that had been written about me. I was so innocent about the press. But I'm learning about this game. My dad was so angry. It hurt him a lot. The story tried to suggest that there was something shady, something unusual about the way my career was being managed just because my family was involved. That implicated Dad directly because he was the one looking after me. The T-shirt thing was taken out of all proportion and thrown in with other bits to make a bigger point about the way my career was being run. He wanted to know how the management side of things ran. How many people were on the Amir Khan payroll? It was another lesson learned. A lesson about trust, and about honesty. I offered both. I'm not sure I got either quality back in return. I was knackered. I tried to do my best. I gave him my time, the opportunity to ask me anything he wanted. I think I deserved better.

I was disappointed, especially for my dad. All he has ever done is the best for his son. I'm not the first professional athlete to be involved in a commercial deal. What was so wrong about wearing a Reebok T-shirt in a photograph? Surely the important thing was that I was there in the first place. For me that was good enough. Not for the *Sunday Times*. I did not let it get to me. I was so angry I instructed solicitors to take action against the *Sunday Times*. We won! The *Sunday Times* published an apology to me and Dad and paid damages which we donated to charity.

I won't let people like that get me down. Even people from his own paper were appalled at the way he had written the story. I have a good relationship with the media. The boxing writers are all good blokes. I've never had a problem with anything they have written. Not all of it has been free of criticism, but it has not been negative. I had not seen this guy before. I'll be ready the next time he comes knocking at my door.

It won't put me off doing what I feel is right. I'm happy with what I have done for the earthquake victims. I realise that I'm not a normal lad any more, that I can use my name to do things for people. If I do stuff, other people get involved. There is still much to do in Pakistan. This was the biggest natural disaster to hit the country. For lots of the survivors the situation is still critical. More public support is now needed to help thousands of people to return to their homes, or what used to be their homes. The agencies want to make sure that when people go back there is proper provision for them, things laid on to help them reconstruct their lives, to rebuild communities and to make sure that if something like this ever happens again they have a better chance of survival.

In the six months after the earthquake first hit more than 1,840 aftershocks were recorded. One of those measured a massive 5.2 on the Richter scale. When you think the original earthquake measured 7.6, it shows you the kind of danger the survivors are still in. Landslides are a massive threat, especially to those who are forced to live in smaller, rough and ready, unofficial camps, where conditions are much worse than in the official camps organised by the aid agencies. Basically the caring never stops. There are always going to be people who need help. Not just in Pakistan but in other poor parts of the world. I'm really switched on to that now.

10

Licence to Thrill

My driving career began in Morrison's car park in Bolton. My mum used to work there part-time on the checkout when I was a kid. Saj took me out in his Daewoo. I was rubbish, clanging the gears, kangarooing all over the place. Like most seventeen year old lads I wanted a car. Saj used to pick me up at the house in Tudor Avenue and take me to college in his. It was cool turning up in a car. It didn't matter much what make it was. You had to have wheels.

Before the Olympics I didn't really have time for driving lessons. When I came back I wanted to sort some out. I didn't have to look far for an instructor. Driving schools in Bolton were queuing up to give me lessons for free. They were hoping to get a bit of exposure out of it, which was fine by me. In the end I went with a company called ADI Driving Force that came to us through Mick. The instructor was called Greg. Like everybody else he was following my story on TV. When he heard that I was seventeen from Bolton and that I trained in Bury, where he lived, he spotted an opportunity. His partner Suzanne got her husband to call Mick. He used to train at Mick's amateur club in Bury. He phoned Mick's home but he was out in Athens with me. The message got through in the end. It's not what you know . . .

It was a smart move by Greg. During the eleven months that it took me to take my test we did loads of media stuff together. We were on *Granada Reports*, in the *Sun* newspaper, stuff like that. The *Granada Reports* thing took about two hours to film. It was the only time I ever messed up a three-point turn. I hit the kerb. After that I tried so hard to do everything right. When it went out on TV they showed only about two minutes. All you could see was me pointing at other drivers, saying, look at him, he's rubbish. They cut out the three-point turn bit. Greg was miffed. He thought his company name would be all over the screen. You never saw it once. He did get a mention by name, though, Greg Kilpatrick, driving instructor. That was cool. It was the same when the *Sun* turned up. Greg thought the company name would be all over the paper. It went in on Christmas Eve. Again there was no mention of his driving school, just Greg Kilpatrick, driving instructor.

Greg had a Renault Megane, a serious step up from Saj's Daewoo. For the first three lessons we went out in Bolton. It was mad. My first lesson was near the test centre next to the bus station. I couldn't drive a car to save my life. I had to learn to start it and stop it without crashing. Every time I stopped the car, which was a lot early on, we were mobbed by people wanting autographs and stuff. Greg could not believe it. He had never seen anything like it. The car was swamped. When they had finished with me they went over to Greg to get his business card. They wanted to be taught by the instructor that showed Amir Khan how to drive.

We had to move the lessons over to Bury after that. I never had another lesson in Bolton. For the first two trips Greg drove to Bury. Then it was down to me. I picked it up really quick. My clutch control was super slick. After about six lessons I was doing everything, three-point turns, reversing, no problem. The only thing I couldn't get at first was the emergency stop. Greg said my first attempt was the longest in history. It went on for about 100 metres. I couldn't bring myself to slam on the brakes.

It didn't feel right. It felt like I was wrecking the car. Once I had sorted that out I was away.

Greg reckons I could have passed my test within three months. But it was mad then. I had just come back from Athens. My life had been turned upside down. I was attending functions, training and fighting in the ABAs, flying off to Cuba, preparing for the Kindelan fight, and then I turned pro. I couldn't fit everything in. I used to practise on my own with my dad or Taz. When I bought my Range Rover I was out all the time. Me and Saj cruising around Bolton with the L-plates on, windows down, music pumping. Mad it was. I used to see Greg loads of times around Bolton out on a lesson. I loved that. I'd pip the horn, all right, Greg, check this out. Greg used to bury his face in his hands. Calm down, Amir, you haven't passed your test yet. Later, Greg, later, I would shout. I'll give you a ring. They say you need about forty hours with an instructor and about thirty practising privately. When I took my test I had been out with Greg twenty times maximum. I lost count of the number of times I was out with Saj.

Since I started with Greg about seven of my mates have been with him, including my cousin Rakeb and my sister Tabinda's husband, Gohar. That was an experience for Greg. Gohar had a licence from Pakistan. When you come to England they give you an international licence that lasts for a year, then you have to pass a driving test here. Gohar's international licence had two days to run when he went for his test. If he had failed he would have been right in it. Because he'd learned to drive in Pakistan, he only ever used one hand on the steering wheel. It was habit. In Pakistan people always drive with the window down and their arm sticking out. Mirrors don't exist. And when you turn a corner, you don't bother indicating, you beep the horn. Twice to go right and once to go left. All you hear all day long is cars pipping horns. When Gohar got in Greg's car he kept pipping the horn when he turned a corner. He never checked his mirrors.

He only ever used that one hand. At least he was confident, Greg said. He was a quick learner, too, once Greg had persuaded him to use two hands on the wheel and stop pipping. He passed no problem.

I took my test in November 2005, almost a year after my first lesson. Partly because I was doing other things and also because of the theory test. You have to pass the theory part before you can take the practical test. Greg always tells people to get that bit out of the way first because then you can get straight on with the practical. My cousin Rakeb passed his theory three days after having his first lesson. It took me five attempts to pass it. I was cool with the driving. I thought the theory would be easy, too. I didn't take it seriously enough. The test was in two parts, thirty-five questions and then the hazard perception test, which was basically watching fourteen two-minute videos on a computer screen. The videos simulated driving. There was a camera on the dashboard while you travel down the road. If you see something like a kid playing with a ball near the pavement that you think might be a hazard, you have to click the mouse. The quicker you do it the more points you get. I did OK on the hazard test but failed on the questions. You needed to get thirty-one of the thirty-five right. I was always in the twenties. I took it three times in Manchester. I was too embarrassed to go back there so I took it again in Bolton. That time I passed on the questions but missed out by a point on the hazard perception test. After that Tabinda bought me a laptop to practise on. When I went to places like press conferences before fights I would take the laptop. Christmas was coming up. I had to pass. It worked. Fifth time lucky. I took the last theory test in Wigan and passed.

Then came the proper test. I didn't think I was nervous but Greg said my driving was totally different that day. I was asking more questions than normal, obviously stuff that was on my mind. And I was so focused. Every time I came to a roundabout I would double-check things with Greg. When we got to the test centre there were others there taking their tests. There were about seven people in the room. It was very quiet, like sitting in a doctor's waiting room. Everybody was trying to play it cool. Then the examiner came out of his office. Even he was trying to play it cool. Mr Khan, right, what would you like me to call you? It was obvious that he knew who I was. Amir, thanks. OK, would you like to lead me to the car? We did all the checks, under the bonnet, all that stuff. Then off we went. I must have been gone about forty minutes. It felt like five. I thought I had passed. You are never sure. The examiner asked me for my documents, driving licence and theory test certificate. That's when Greg knew I had passed. If you haven't they don't bother.

I was buzzing. Texts were flying off everywhere. My mates knew that Amir Khan would be out there in a sick (top) car. The L-plates were off. I was cruising around Bolton in a Range Rover. When the police see young lads in cars like that they always pull them. I didn't have to wait long for my first 'routine check'. I was buzzing off it because I knew I was clean. It happened near the old house in Tudor Avenue. An Audi TT overtook me. It looked like we were racing. We weren't. I was doing less than 30 mph. Is this your vehicle? Yes, officer. Are you insured? Yes. How old are you? Eighteen. Are you sure you're insured? Yes, honest. Then they check the plates on the radio to make sure it's not stolen. Thank you, Mr Khan, drive safely. I've been pulled a few times. Sometimes, if the policemen recognise me, I give them an autograph. I never take the mickey. They are just doing their job.

Once I had passed my test the world was my oyster. No distance was too short. I used to drive to the end of the street and back just to be seen in the Range Rover. Before I bought my BMW Schnitzer I had some fancy steel alloys put on the Range Rover. Every Thursday I would take it up to a big car park in the centre of Bolton where the boys turned up in their cars. It is a big thing in the area. People come from places like Manchester,

Preston, Oldham and Bury just to show out in their cars. You can have as many as 200 cars up there on a good night. When I first went up there I was with a mate in his Honda. That was before the Olympics when nobody knew who I was. There are loads of Novas, Golfs, Fiestas, Clios, Subarus, cars like that, all done up with nice paint jobs and proper sound systems. You just park up and have a walk around checking out the other cars. When I pulled into the car park in the Range Rover it was like big respect, that's Amir Khan, look at that car. I could see people were a bit shy about coming over, so I used to get out and go over to them, say nice things about their cars. After that everybody just relaxed. When I go up there now, I know most of the faces. I just chill in the Schnitzer. I have taken the alloys off the Range Rover. That went down well with my dad.

11

Boyz in the Hood

As a professional sportsman I could probably live anywhere I wanted. London is the obvious place that comes up in conversation. People assume that as a young lad with a few quid I'd be off to the Smoke in search of a good time, invest in property and live the fancy life. That's not me. Bolton knocks spots off London for me. People say hello to you in the street. I'm recognised wherever I go. Not in a horrible way. Just a nod, all right, Amir? That kind of stuff. It's cool people knowing who you are. London is just too busy, traffic everywhere. You get into the rhythm of a place. I've never got into the rhythm of London. I can see that it is nice. I usually stay in a hotel on Park Lane. Very nice. But it's not home. Bolton is all I have known. You probably wouldn't choose to live here if you did not know it. I accept that. But for me, it's in my blood. It has chosen me. I'm glad for that. There are 275,000 people living in Bolton. I wouldn't say I know them all. But they all know me.

You kind of take a place for granted. I travelled around as an amateur all over the country. As a professional I do it a bit differently, in planes instead of cars. It makes the world a smaller place in a way. The one thing that hasn't changed is the feeling coming back to Bolton. As soon as I see the signs for the M61 I can smell my mum's cooking. I can feel the atmosphere changing. In a weird way, I feel like I'm coming back to myself, the real

Amir, the Amir that my mates know and my family. I'm the same boy everywhere but only in Bolton can I truly be myself. I know that is not unique. Everybody has a place they call home. Bolton is mine. Bolton means different things to the people that live here. My Bolton is not Vernon Kay's Bolton. Not Sam Allardyce's Bolton. Not Peter Kay's Bolton. I've never met Peter Kay. He is probably the most famous person in the town. Our paths don't cross. I have met his mate, Paddy McGuinness. He's cool, a really nice guy. He's been to one of my fights. But for me Bolton is about hanging out with my mates.

Saj is my top mate. He never sees the celebrity Amir. To him I was always the lad he met in college. He knows everything about me, the good things and the bad. He's a chiller, a top lad. He does not want anything from me. When we met he was the one with all the tools, the car, everything. After the Olympics I did not see him for a week. He did not want to intrude. He's my right-hand man. Whenever people ask me for my phone number I give them Saj's. He gets calls every day. He phoned me one day and said, Amir, you've just had a call from the toughest man in the world. It was Joe Egan, the Irish boxer who wrote a book about his life in the fight game. I like Joe, he's a nice lad. He was cool about it. He had a chat with Saj instead.

Saj works the morning shift at a call centre in Bolton. The rest of the time he chills with me. We rip each other all the time. I'm always digging him about the size of his head. It's massive. My ears stick out. He calls me satellite dish. Saj is my shopping partner. Whenever I go to the Trafford Centre or somewhere like that, Saj is on the trip. He's my decoy. We always have a laugh. He goes into the changing room to try a top, say. I wait outside on my own. By the time he comes out, I'm mobbed by people wanting autographs.

In one shop, River Island at the Trafford Centre, the shop assistant came running towards me. Ah, Amir Khan. You are a top boxer. I've seen all your fights. He was an Asian lad from

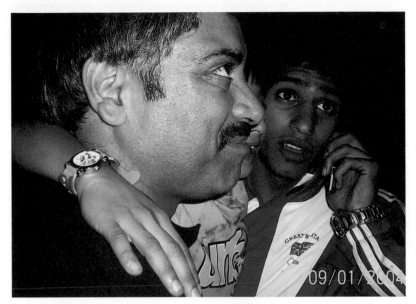

Mad return home after the Olympics! Being mobbed at Manchester Airport

My last amateur fight: the rematch against Kindelan in May 2005

Signing my pro contract with Frank Warren in July 2005

© Bolton Colour Labs

© Mirrorpix

Taking a break at Oliver's Gym

Coming into the ring for my first pro fight

© Getty Images Sport

With my cousin, Lancashire and England cricketer Saj Mahmood

With my mate Saj on a trip to Bulgaria to watch Liverpool in the Champions League final

Backstage at GMTV (left to right): Asif, Jordan, friend Gareth Williams, me and Peter Andre

At a 2006 charity appeal for victims of the Pakistan earthquake, with Majid, Uncle Taz and Dad

Posing with Ricky Hatton, WBA welterweight champion

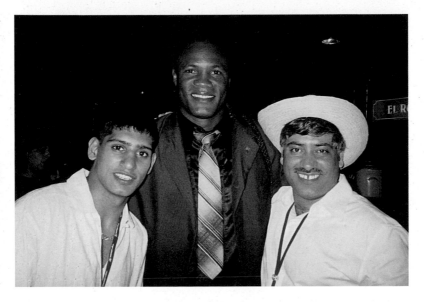

The Cuban greats: meeting Felix Savon with Dad (above)
and meeting Teofilo Stevenson with Kindelan (below)

Posing in front of my car

Me and my mates at Queen's Park after a football game

Visiting Muzaffarabad after the earthquake in Pakistan in 2005

One of my school visits, signing autographs for schoolkids

With my family in 2006 (clockwise from bottom left): Haroon, me, Gohar (my brother-in-law), Mum, Dad, my niece Hadia, Tabinda and Mariyah

Nelson. He said, let me give you something. I thought he was talking about a discount. He put his hand in his pockets and brought out a handful of £20 notes. I said I can't take that. I don't want it. He said, no, no, you have to have it. I looked at Saj. It is traditional in the Asian community to hand over gifts or cash in this way. He was raising his eyebrows as if to say, take it. I had no choice. The lad scrunched the notes up in a ball and shoved them in my pocket. He said, at least you will remember me now wherever you go. We do as well. We counted up the notes outside. There was £200.

Saj is almost as famous as me in Bolton. When we went to Blackpool for his birthday, there was a picture of us the next day in the *Sun*, our eyes popping out on one of the rides at the Pleasure Beach. Everywhere we went in Bolton we were getting ripped about that picture. They should have seen us in the Terror House. That scared me to death. You had this guy chasing you around with a chain saw. We laughed about it on the outside but when you are in there you think it's for real. When we walked through the door we were all tough lads. Soon as we got inside we stuck together like babies. Saj was saying, Amir, you go first, you are the boxer. You had to knock on a door to go into another room. No one would knock on it. At one point I went flying through an exit door and ended up in a bar with normal people having a drink. They thought I was some sort of crazy freak. I had a wild look on my face. It was mad in that house.

Saj is my Jimmy Five Bellies, Gazza's mate. I just feel better having Saj around. It's mad being a celebrity. Sometimes it's good just to have a mate with you. It keeps things normal. Whenever I get invited to stuff I take Saj with me. He came to the Champions League Final in Istanbul to watch Liverpool. ITV sorted that out. We had top seats. Every time Liverpool scored people jumped on Saj. We stayed a couple of days after the match, haggling in the Grand Bazaar. Saj saw a watch he liked. The bloke wanted $400 – about £220. Saj was going to pay it. I beat him down so much he wanted us to take it for free. It was a Breitling. A copy. Saj paid £20 for it in the end. Some stuff was rubbish. But there were lots of proper bargains, leather bags, rugs, stuff that costs you a fortune at home. I remember we were given rugs at one England boxing tournament. A lot of the lads left them behind. One lad took his to a shop when he got home and had it valued – £600. The others were crying. I bought loads of stuff for the family. I always come back with more than I go with. From Dubai I came back with a massive globe for my mum and dad. It's got pride of place in the front room at the new house.

Dubai was a laugh. I took the full crew out there. The Bolton boys on tour for six days. There were about fifteen of us. The jet-ski bloke won't be inviting us back. We wrecked four of his machines. Complete write-offs. They were like motorbikes on the water. Really powerful. None of us really knew how to control them. Taz crashed his into my mate Maj. Maj couldn't swim. Taz had to dive in to rescue him. He had his phone in his pocket, and loads of money. It was wild. We were there for six days. I needed that time. It was a chance to hang out with my mates in a place where not many people knew me. I got recognised a bit, in bars and restaurants, but nothing like home. At home it has become practically impossible to go anywhere and not be noticed. When I go into shops people won't let me pay for anything. They are always trying to give me stuff. It sounds OK but when it is happening to you all the time it gets a bit embarrassing. You dream about the times when you could do what you wanted, go to places without any fuss. There is no way I can go into Bolton town centre on a Saturday during the day like I used to.

On the other side of the coin certain opportunities present themselves that I would never have had otherwise. I got to know Andy Murray at the Sports Personality of the Year Awards. That was cool. He is a good lad. He's going through similar things to me. He just wants to go out and play tennis. When he does every shot, every serve is talked about, analysed. You feel like your life is not your own. We got on well. He likes his boxing. He came to one of my fights in Glasgow. A couple of weeks later he came to Oliver's gym to do a training session with me. He found it really hard. We messed him up a bit. He understands now how hard a sport boxing is. It is not just what happens on fight night. Getting hit is bad enough, but you need strength, stamina, speed, skill and technique to get on. To get them you need to spend a lot of time in the gym. At Oliver's we put him on the bar for two minutes. It nearly killed him.

There has been a lot of talk about Andy's fitness levels. I'm no tennis expert but from what I saw in the gym he could definitely be fitter. He was strong, though. You could feel it in his punches. The press want to watch it. The next time they get out of line with him he might let them have it. He worked out for an hour. The next time I'll do something on his turf. I fancy a bit of tennis. Maybe he can get me into Wimbledon. I've never been there.

Meeting people like Andy has been great. It's not the real world, though. I need Bolton to keep me grounded. My life is based around boxing. It is my life. My days are mapped out around training, my weeks around fights. When I approach a fight I get snappy. All fighters do when they are peaking. They want things their own way. About two weeks out I start to go through the odd mood swing. It's about preparing to fight. That's when you need your mates most. They get some grief from me but they know how to handle it. You just want to lash out all the time, get rid of some aggression. When I'm like that they tell me it's my time of the month.

Since I turned pro in July 2005, I've had fights about every couple of months. I'm still adjusting to that rhythm. In a way it was much more fun as an amateur. You were part of a team then. Whenever I fought I was always surrounded by team-mates and coaches. We'd travel together, fight together, chill together. You always had someone to talk to, things in common to worry about, opponents, referees, judges. As a pro I can't share the pressure with my team, with another lad stood next to me going through the same thing, feeling the same pressure. Oliver is always there, trying to keep things nice and level around fight time, but that pressure is always there because I'm the one throwing and taking the punches. Fighters are the only ones who know what that's like. It's like no other feeling in the world.

Dealing with these things on my own for the first time has been a massive learning curve. And I've been doing it at a time in my life when things are changing. I've been kind of maturing, growing into a man in public. That's a strange thing to do. Being a teenager is tough anyway at times. Being famous is weird. I'm just glad that I found boxing. I know that without it I would have had a very different life. Boxing has given my life shape. I've had to work hard for everything. When people see me in the ring it looks effortless. It's not. It has taken blood, sweat and tears to get where I am. And this is just the start.

The money has been great. It has changed our lives. It's nice to be able to buy things that you could never afford before. Getting my BMW was brilliant. All my mates are into cars. We grew up arguing about which car we would buy if we won the Lottery. It was a privilege to be able to do that. And getting the house. I never thought I'd be able to buy my own house at this stage in my life. Kids of eighteen and nineteen just can't do that. I looked at a few places then settled on a house everybody liked. It's a bungalow, actually. We've already added an extension. Next year I'm planning to build an annexe just for me and my mates to chill in. A boys' house with a games room, TV screen, PlayStation. No girls allowed. The house is perfect. It's in a nice part of Bolton, off the main road. It has electric gates, which are brilliant for privacy. I loved the old house at Tudor Avenue, but it was getting mad over there. People would just stroll up to the house, knock on the door and ask for pictures and autographs. We all outgrew it. I'll never outgrow Bolton.

Whenever I'm away at a press conference or a fight I like to jump in the car as soon as I get home and hit the hood, check out the scene, see what's happening. There are certain places where the boys meet, usually around 5 p.m. to 5.30. The forecourt of the Shell garage at the back of Chorley Old Road or the tennis courts in Queen's Park. If they are not in one place they are definitely at the other. When we were kids we would meet on foot. My brother does that now. These days we cruise in cars. I still do my sprints now in Queen's Park. On the other side of the park from the tennis courts there is a path with massive trees either side that leads down a hill to the park gate. I sprint up that path on Saturday mornings. Normally I do six sets of five shuttles. On the last set I carry on running up the hill past the trees and over to my car parked by the tennis courts. That keeps me so fit. By the time I get back to my car I'm breathing really heavily. It feels good. Those tennis courts are exactly the same now as they have always been. They've got wire fencing all around to keep the balls in. We never played tennis. We just sat on the bench at the back under the trees and chilled. In the summer we would be there for hours, checking the scene, having a laugh, ripping each other about clothes, haircuts and personal stuff. My ears always end up getting a mention on that bench.

Sometimes I take myself off to a few old places, like the Halliwell gym. Though the old gym is not there any more a new one has opened above it. It's great to see young kids in there, keeping fit, learning the ropes. It's very neat and tidy. Personally I preferred the old place. I loved the smell of that gym, the feel of it. It felt like a place where people should fight. Oliver's gym in Salford is the same, beat up, lived in, a proper place to train. Outside the old Halliwell gym it's just the same. The same fencing on the houses opposite and the same cobbles on the street.

I was brought up not far from the old gym. We lived in a kind of cul-de-sac behind Brownlow Fold Junior School, where I was asked to leave as a kid. Our house backed on to Uncle Terry's. He still lives there. It is a nice, quiet area. Not much traffic so the kids can play out safely. We used to be out all the time. Saj would get the cricket bat out and all the cousins would be in there bowling and batting until it went dark. Sometimes we would play in Brownlow Fold playground. There is a picture of a fire extinguisher painted on the wall. We used to use that as the wickets. When the ball went on the roof I was always the one climbing up there to get it down. I was like Spiderman. For big matches we would play on the field around the corner. We had a corky ball, pads, wickets, the lot. It was all Saj's stuff. He has always had the kit. All the family would turn up, aunties, uncles, everybody.

Halliwell Road is the area where the key men hang out. That's our patch. My boys are tops. I drive over there every fortnight to get a haircut. The guy who does it, Shiraz or Siz for short, is Indian. Saj is Indian, too. We are driving race relations forward in Bolton. Siz is cool. Half the people that go in his shop are white. That's unusual for Asian barbers. Siz is an old mate of Taz's from school. He has been cutting my hair since he opened his shop Kool Kutz five years ago. Apart from Dad we all go in there, Taz, Harry, cousin Saj. I used to come straight from school in my uniform and wait my turn. Siz would always ask me about my amateur fights. He has followed my career from his barber's chair. When I'm fighting I go there four days before the bout. Siz is a top barber. I need to look my best to fight my best. It's part of the ritual. It's as crucial to me as packing my kit bag, part of my preparation. As soon as I start to put the towel in the bag, put the gum shield in, the bandages, boxing boots, foul guard, I am mentally getting ready to fight. Plus, I know that I haven't forgotten anything. Taz bought me a poncho once. I wore it from fight number seven onwards, when

I moved to Bury ABC. After one bout in Liverpool we left it to Harry to pack everything up. He forgot it. Easily done. Now I never leave it to anyone else.

It's the same with my hair. It has to be right. I don't care what anybody says. If I know I'm looking good, my kit is good, the gloves feel good, I box well. If your kit is too big or too small or the gloves are crap it's no good. I boxed in some places as an amateur when the foam in the glove came out in my hands. All that was left was the leather. Mad.

I never grow my hair too long anyway. I like it short. It looks sharper. And maybe that 0.0004 of a second faster it makes me could be the difference. I might get caught with a punch otherwise. Being a boxer is not like being a footballer. You don't see boxers with big hair like Beckham. We don't do funky. Siz knows just how I like it. He gives me a ring when he can fit me in. He opens his shop up especially. Obviously he can't do it during normal opening hours any more because the moment I take my seat, the place gets banged out. Once he rang me at 10.30 at night. It was the only shop with lights on at that time of night. Siz had the clippers in his hands ready.

The last time I popped in I had a little kid in tears. It wasn't my fault. He goes in there with his dad, a Chinese kid. He's only about six or seven. Every time he goes in he asks Siz if I've been in, too, and when I might be coming back. He's one of my biggest fans. After the Komjathi fight in Belfast I was driving past the shop. I was with Haroon and Saj on a cruise around town. When I walked in the lad's eyes were out on stalks. The shop was full of people. It was just after school so a lot of mums and dads were in with their kids. Siz shouts out to the lad, look who's here. Because the shop was packed he was too embarrassed to speak to me. He dived behind his dad on the bench. We couldn't get him out of there. I dropped a signed photo into the shop to say sorry. And he got his haircut for free. He'll be able to tell that story for the rest of his life.

Another time I had a photo shoot lined up for early afternoon. I decided at the last minute that I needed a trim. I called Siz. While I was on the line he asked the people waiting if they would mind if he slipped me in ahead of them. No problem, they said. In the end I got delayed. Siz cut their hair anyway but none of them would go home afterwards. They all stayed because they wanted to see me. Siz reckons he gets quite a bit of business on the back of cutting my hair. He's had a few lads in from *Coronation Street* and one from *Hollyoaks*. He didn't recognise them, though. He doesn't watch much TV.

My style has not changed much over the years. It's a bit shorter now than it used to be. Taz is the one who goes for the big styles. Siz reckons he does it to cover up his grey hairs. Saj likes a funky cut, too. Because he's been off with England a lot he has been letting it go lately. During the World Cup it got like a mop. Siz sorted him out. He gave him a mullet.

Opposite my mate's barber's shop is a car-hire place. I'm not talking Avis or Hertz. I'm talking serious motors here: Ferraris, Porsches, BMWs, CLRs. Lads hire them for weddings to look cool, or just for the weekend. They pay £700 or £800 for a couple of days, drive them around town with the roof down looking sharp. It's mad, a big scene among the Asian lads in Bolton. I don't know how they do it. I drive my car around with the roof down but I don't have to watch my back. These are my wheels. People want that image. Some lads might have cars worth £60,000 and houses worth £40,000. Saj lives over on the south side of town, Derby Street. That's a big Indian Muslim community. It's cool over there, like Green Street in East London on a Saturday. Buzzing. We go over there a lot. There are clothes shops, restaurants, takeaways. The food is great. The boys look after us. I pull up outside in the car, Saj jumps out and places the order. Nasser is the man in there. He gives us a big discount. He usually charges us a pound a head for food and a drink. Basically he gives it away. I had five of us in my car the other day. It cost a fiver to feed all of us. Great chicken kebabs, too. Not any old rubbish. You wouldn't get that in London. It's almost as good as Moods, my auntie's curry place in the centre of town. I opened it with cousin Saj in January. I go round there and help out sometimes, work on the till taking money. People come in and whisper to each other, is that Amir Khan on that till? We have a good laugh in there.

Considering the start I made in life, running my parents ragged, it's a miracle that I've not had that much contact with policemen. I have had my moments though. The most recent was in my new car, the convertible BMW, in the centre of Bolton. It was my first accident; I was involved in a collision with a pedestrian. I didn't know what to do. I wasn't bothered about the car. That could be replaced. I was concerned about the guy. There were loads of people who saw what had happened. People were speaking up for me, telling others what had happened. By the time the police arrived the scene was crowded with people. There was even a photographer snapping away. People were asking me for autographs and stuff. It wasn't the right time. The police advised me to sit in the back of their car to get out of the mêlée. Within an hour the story was being reported on the local TV news.

The next day there were photos in the *Daily Mirror* and the *Sun* of me sitting in the police car, ringed for dramatic effect, and of my car being lifted on to a tow truck. I learned a lot from that afternoon. It showed me that fame and celebrity are no protection when something like that happens. For an hour or two I was just another ordinary citizen, the focus of a police inquiry into a traffic incident. It was shocking for me. I was supposed to be fighting in Glasgow a couple of weeks later. Luckily the bill was scrapped. Until then everything had been going like a dream for me. That showed me how things can happen when you least expect them. How quickly you can be brought back to earth. The next day I got my dad to phone the hospital to check the man was OK. We also spoke to his family. It turned out he was a boxing fan, a big fan of mine.

Before that, just after I had returned from my first attempt to qualify for the Olympics, there was a knock at the door. We were still at the old house in Tudor Avenue. My dad answered. It was a policeman. He wanted to ask me some questions about an incident in Vernon Street, Bolton. Some guy had accused me and Ricky Hatton of beating him up on the day after I got back from Croatia. I didn't have a clue what he was on about. It was frightening, a shock to me.

The policeman asked me loads of questions. It was like a bad movie. Where were you at such a time on such a day? Who were you with? What were you doing? I know the police have a job to do, to investigate allegations, but it was hassle I could have done without. I was worried in case it came out. Stories like that can be very damaging. The guy claimed that he had recognised me from a Ricky Hatton fight. I got into the ring with Ricky and touched gloves. He told the police that he recognised me and Ricky from that fight. It was absolute rubbish, but the policeman said when he left the house that he would have to take the matter further. I didn't really know what he meant by that. It didn't come to anything. I can't remember where Ricky said he was but it wasn't Bolton. He could prove it easily. And so could I. It wasn't as if I have ever chilled with Ricky. I don't really know him socially.

The only incident that produced a stain on my record happened just after I had finished school before going to the Junior Olympics in America. I was in Queen's Park as usual, hanging out with a few lads. Harry was there, too, on his bike. He must have been about eleven or twelve. A load of girls were in the park. They were obviously drunk. There must have been about ten or so of them. Most of them were under age. They started getting abusive, calling us names. I was with some nutty mates that day. They sent Harry off on his bike to get some eggs. When he came back they started chasing the girls with the eggs. I didn't get involved with that. It was nothing to do with me. I had been in loads of situations like that before where I've had to step back when trouble started. There is too much at stake for me, a boxer, getting involved in scuffles in the street. I recognised one of the girls from Smithills School. I think that was what got me into trouble. I'd even seen her after it happened. She never said anything to me about it.

Then, a couple of months after the incident, the police came around to the house. It was a big hassle for me. One of the girls said her skirt had been lifted. If it had been I never saw it. I was there but not involved. I couldn't prove that I didn't do anything. Obviously eggs were thrown by someone. But not me. I'm not sure any of the girls were hit with the eggs. None of those lads who were there spoke up for me. They knew what had happened but nobody wanted to take the blame. So we were all blamed. I had to go to the police station to make statements, to give my side of events. In the end it went to court and I was convicted of affray. It's only a minor offence but it still hurt. Harry got done for getting the eggs. If bigger lads tell you to go and get something, you do it.

I maintained my innocence throughout. My profile was building. I knew how damaging something like this could be. I didn't want a conviction on my record. I didn't do anything. I was in the wrong place at the wrong time. I have not spoken to any of those lads since. I think the police sympathised with me. The court stated that the conviction would come off my record after twelve months if there were no further incidents. It was very upsetting for Mum and Dad. They believed me but that didn't change the outcome. It was another lesson learned. I woke up that day. I'm very careful who I hang with now. It's a shame really. I still don't think there was any malice in what happened. Every kid in England can hold his hand up to mischief. In most cases it never gets a mention.

These days I have to be more careful. My boys know that I can't do any silly stuff. They look after me in a way those other kids didn't. They make adjustments. Chilling is still chilling. It has to be done. I just have to be more wary. I want to be remembered for the good things I have done not the daft things. Hopefully the gym I'm building will help. It will be my own landmark in Bolton. I'm putting down a marker in cement.

We bought an old building just behind the office in St George's Road. The plan is for it to be up and running by the end of the year. I'll move my training operation there from Oliver's gym in Salford. It won't take long to re-create the atmosphere we have down there. Half of it will be a pro gym, the other half for amateurs. We'll have an amateur coach there looking after the youngsters coming through. It will be a place for kids to come and get a feel for boxing. There are not enough proper boxing facilities in Bolton for youngsters. Since I flagged it up on my website we've had loads of inquiries from girls as well as boys. The demand is out there. I want to help meet it. I'm really proud of it. It's not about making money. The subs will only be 50p or a pound to train. On Fridays, when I go into the office after prayers at the mosque, there are loads of emails and letters about it.

I want kids of nine and ten to get excited about boxing like I did. To enjoy a sport that teaches you proper lessons about how to get on in life. Not everybody is going to make it to the Olympics, but the kids that stick with it will learn how to look after themselves, how to make the most of what they have. If the gym achieves that, I will have given something positive back to Bolton.

12

7 July 2005

On 7 July 2005, nine days before my pro debut, three young Muslim lads strapped bombs to their backs and blew themselves and three London Underground trains to bits. A fourth blew up a bus. A total of fifty-six people died and 700 were injured. It was the worst terrorist act in London since the Second World War. And overnight it turned me, a young boxer from Bolton, into a political figure. I became a spokesman for Asian youth. Like me, three of those lads were of Pakistani descent. One of them, Hasib Hussain, was exactly the same age: eighteen. It was mad.

The pressure was on me big time with my first pro fight just days away. But all of a sudden the picture had changed. People wanted to ask me about the bombings. Politically I didn't want anything to do with it. I'm a boxer, a sportsman. What did I know about politics? How should I know why four young lads would want to kill themselves and loads of innocent people? I couldn't imagine why anybody would want to do that. At the same time I realised that I was in a unique position. I was famous. I was Asian. And I was more or less the same age as the terrorists. I had no choice. If I turned away from that situation people might have thought that I was just like them, that I thought like them, that I hated the British people and the government like they did, that I sympathised with them and their 'cause'. I didn't want to put that message across. Those people did not represent me. I don't want people like that to represent me. I would never associate with those kinds of people. They were wrong. Brainwashed. You couldn't class them as human beings, never mind British.

I had to respond. I wanted to respond. It was back to that responsibility thing again. If the bombs had gone off a year before, no one would have been asking me anything. Now I was the most famous Asian lad in Britain. People were looking to me for clues as to why people might do something as mad as that. I had no answers. All I could do was stand up and tell the world that not all Asian lads grow up to be crazy terrorists and killers. I might look like them, culturally I was linked to them but in reality I had more in common with the victims. It could have been me down there. I spent a lot of time in tube stations going to England camps and stuff. Like the majority of those that lost their lives that day I was a British citizen going about my business.

On the night of the fight I walked out with the British flag. I wanted to show people that Asian lads like me were proud to be British. All my mates in the crowd had a massive flag, half Union Jack and half Pakistani, with the slogan Knock Out Terrorism written on it. The bloke who made it for them did it for free. He was white. I dedicated the fight to the victims. The crowd responded brilliantly. Since then, wherever I have fought the crowds have been great. Since then everybody gets behind me. It doesn't matter where they come from, what race they are or what religion they believe in. They call out my name. That makes me so proud. That night in Bolton it made me more proud than ever. I was fighting a white English lad, yet the crowd were shouting for me. About 7 per cent of people in Bolton are Asian Muslim. I have never known anybody speak about or be involved in mad talk about blowing people up. As a kid growing up in Bolton, racism was never a problem. I never once felt that I didn't belong. We don't think of ourselves as different. Yes, we are obviously of Asian origin, from Pakistan, but that does not separate us from our neighbours. We are just from Bolton. It has always been like that. Whenever I go to Pakistan I'm happy to say I'm from England. That's how it is. That's how I feel.

Looking back, the fight fell at the right time. I recognised in the days after the London bombings just how powerful a symbol Amir Khan was becoming. I learned that I could use my name, my fame to raise awareness about lots of things. I could put messages in people's heads. Stop terrorism, things like that. A year on I feel that really strongly. I have a platform now. I can make a difference in a way others can't. That is a huge responsibility. Massive. I'm no longer just a fighter. I did not choose that role, but I accept it. I'm not frightened of it. People listen to me. After the fight all the papers reported what I had said. There was twice as much written about my debut because of what had happened in London. That's the way it is. At least it was positive coverage of a Muslim boy.

Every day the papers and news programmes are full of negative stories from all over the world about Muslims. It is no wonder people think we all go around killing people, blowing people up, Iraq, Afghanistan, every day the same. But that is so far away from the experience of the vast majority of people of the Muslim faith. In the Islamic religion it is a sin to take your own life, never mind anybody else's. For me religion is an entirely personal thing. It's about spiritual guidance. My uncle Terry sums it up best. He says that if he can get to the end of his life without having caused anyone any harm or pain then he will have lived a good life, been a good man, a good Muslim. There is no need to be scared of people who worship Islam. I was born into the faith. I believe in Allah. But I understand that others might see the world differently. I respect absolutely their right to believe what they want. To practise whatever religion they choose. What's the problem?

Because of what is happening in certain parts of the world people have come to see Muslims as religious maniacs, people to fear. This is the opposite of the everyday reality of Muslims. Islam is a peaceful religion. Yet when you turn on the TV you only hear about the fighting, the bombs, the deaths. You see pictures of men in beards carrying guns, talking about holy wars, jihad. What happened in America in 2001 changed everything in lots of ways. For Muslims in Britain it made things very awkward. I was too young to understand it, but I was aware that it was a big thing. It was talked about in the mosque, the religious leaders put out statements. It was happening on TV screens in Bolton and the rest of Britain. It was New York. People were saying London would be next. It put the Asian community on the spot in a way.

It was the same with the London bombings. This time I was a little bit older and in a totally different position. I know what it felt like for me, people looking to me to say something, to make sense of a mad situation for them. That is how it must have been for the Muslim leaders after 9/11. You feel responsible in a way, when really it has nothing to do with you. It is a bit like the situation in Northern Ireland. Just because Christians are fighting each other in that part of the world, Protestants and Catholics, it doesn't mean that Protestants and Catholics are like that everywhere.

If people knew more about Islam and what it is to be a Muslim in Britain, they would soon realise that there is nothing to be scared of. The Islamic holy book, the Koran, preaches peace and respect. As far as I understand it, there is nowhere in the Koran that tells you it is OK to kill. It's exactly the opposite. You cannot commit a greater sin than to take an innocent life. That message is drummed into us from an early age, at least it was in our case. In Bolton all the Muslim kids have to study the Koran. From the age of seven I had to go to the mosque to read the holy book from back to front. Literally. In Arabic books always start at the back and work forward. I know lots of people who are Christian, Church of England or whatever, and have never read the Bible. They might know the odd story or parable, but not many kids these days have read the Bible all the way through. We had to do that.

It was the same mosque that my dad and his brothers attended, the Medina Mosque in St George's Road in Bolton, one of the first to be built in the town. When my dad started going there, it was one of only three mosques in Bolton. Now there are about sixteen. Some in the Muslim community think that is too many. In a way it is a sign of how multicultural Bolton has become. St George's Road is right in the town centre. Opposite the mosque is Claremont Church. On the wall of the church there is a big sign that says 'one church, one Lord, worship him here'. That shows you how people of different faiths can live together happily. It has always been like that for us in Bolton.

The Medina Mosque is basically two terraced houses at the end of the street knocked through to make one building. Inside the rooms are converted into classrooms, and a large hall. There is also a big shower room for people to cleanse their bodies. One for women, another for men. It is very important to be cleansed before prayer. It is a symbol of purity. It is part of the ritual, part of the discipline. It has to be right, like taping the hands in boxing. Unless you wrap the hands properly you can't fight. As kids we would mostly wash at home after school. The adults who go to the mosque straight from work use the shower room, which has small stools arranged in a line in front of lots of taps. You basically sit on the stools and wash your whole body.

Like churches, mosques are obviously sacred places. You couldn't mess about in there. I knew as soon as I walked in I had to behave. There was none of the usual naughty stuff I used to get up to as a five-year-old in school. If I did I would get a stick across my knuckles. The imam used to hold it in his hand ready to pounce. There would be as many as 300 children associated with that one mosque. The boys and girls studied in different rooms. The first thing you do when you enter a mosque is take off your shoes. If you need to wash you go in the shower room, then you go to the prayer room to pray. It doesn't look anything like the inside of a church. It is basically a big, empty space.

The floor of the Medina is carpeted like a house. On the walls there are various pictures of religious places like Mecca and stuff. And there are sayings taken from the Koran written on paper and stuck on the wall; erase old sins with new virtues, things like that. Along the walls there are bookcases containing religious works. The Koran is split up into thirty smaller books. On one wall by the main window is a special clock showing the traditional prayer times. Muslims are supposed to pray five times a day at the mosque. The first prayer is at 4.10 a.m. The last is at 10.50 p.m. Obviously not everybody goes to the mosque five times a day. When the Koran was written it was easier to divide the day around prayer. These days it is acceptable to pray anywhere, but it is better if you can do it at the mosque.

As kids we had to change into traditional clothes, the shalwar kameez, to study at the mosque, and wear a tiny cap. We knelt down at small benches in rows. They were quite low to the ground so you couldn't get your legs under. There were about ten boys to a bench. It was not easy. The Koran is written in Arabic. Most of the kids came from families that spoke Urdu and Punjabi. I understood a bit of Urdu but I spoke English. But at seven I barely knew how to read in English, never mind Arabic. There are translations of the Koran into other languages but for the purposes of studying it as a scripture you have to read it in Arabic. That meant learning Arabic first.

It takes most kids about three to four years to learn Arabic and to complete the Koran. That is four years of coming to the mosque every day after school for two hours. Basically you sit in a class with the imam, who is like a priest. The imam explains things, then you read the words out loud. Every single one of them. It helps with the understanding of the holy book if the Arabic is pronounced properly. It was tough, but we all did it so no one used to think anything of it. It was just another part of our school day. The only real break you get is during Ramadan. Because I got into boxing just after I started to read the Koran it took me a bit longer than my mates to get to the end. When you have finished the Koran some kids stay on to learn Urdu properly. That's what I did. I finished when I was about fifteen.

When you have read the holy book you are expected to follow its principles throughout life. That means praying to Allah five times a day. I do that sometimes but not at the mosque. Like lots of people it is not possible for me to get to the mosque every day. The most important day is Friday. Friday prayers are like church on Sunday for the Christian faith. The imam leads the prayers and then he usually chooses a small passage of the Koran to discuss as part of the service. It takes about an hour, between one and two in the afternoon. I always try to make that when I can.

I consider myself a religious person. It is very important to me. I believe in my God, Allah, and try to follow his teachings. Basically that means being a good human being, helping others. Nothing more complicated than that. It's not mad or weird, just normal stuff. Since 9/11 Muslim religious leaders in the mosques have been careful to send out a clear message about terrorism. At the Medina Mosque in Bolton terrorism has been condemned many times. It is just wrong. The majority of imams everywhere are preaching that message. No extremist views are expressed. There are committees that monitor all imams. After 9/11 the committees paid even greater attention to the teachings of the imams to ensure that kids were not getting the wrong message. That fits into the way I think about the world. I am not a religious expert. I do not study the Koran every day, trying to interpret its teachings. That is the job of the imams.

I know that imams in different parts of the world disagree on certain things. That is part of the problem. The Koran is used in many ways to justify all sorts of things. It gets very complicated at that level and very political. I'm not used to all that stuff. I'm an English lad, a boxer trying to be a world champion. I don't know what it is like in places like Iraq or Iran or Afghanistan. I don't know if kids there grow up learning the Koran as I did. People with more experience and knowledge of these things reckon that a lot of these kids can't read or write. They grow up in these remote mountain places believing what they are told. If they are told bad things then you can see why they turn out like they do. They do not know any different. Under extreme regimes like the Taliban in Afghanistan kids grow up hating people in the West because that is what they are told. But that is not the experience of most practising Muslims in the world. It is not what I was taught in Bolton. I did not grow up'hating Westerners. I am a Westerner. I was taught to respect everybody, no matter what race or religion they were. Muslims in Britain are ordinary working people just like everyone else. There is nothing for ordinary people to fear in Islam. There is nothing strange or unusual about it. And there is no need to be wary of ordinary Muslims.

It was funny. During the World Cup there were loads of Asians driving around Bolton with English flags on their cars. My dad's mate, Sabir, is married to a pharmacist. Her shop is on Deane Road in a part of the town where lots of Indian Muslims live. The Indian Muslims and the Bangladeshi Muslims stick more to traditional dress. The men all wear the shalwar kameez, hats and long beards, some of the women wear burqas. I think it is because in their countries Muslims are a minority. They wear more traditional stuff to emphasise their Muslim identity. That carried over when they moved to England.

But even in that part of Bolton the English flag was out during the World Cup. It comes from the kids, the younger generation, people like me. Things are changing. But there is still much to be done to change perceptions. I have been given a role in that process. Sport allows me to reach every part of the community in a way politicians can't. I'm a hero for young kids no matter what their colour or creed. Winning an Olympic silver medal in a British vest made sure of that. I'm proud to be in this position, an Asian lad changing minds, a normal lad from a normal family. I'm not interested in politics, but I am interested in making a difference if I can.

My favourite fighter is Muhammad Ali. When I used to watch videos of him as a kid when I first started boxing, all I saw were the brilliant moves, the *Rumble in the Jungle* with George Foreman, the *Thriller in Manila* against Joe Frazier. I wanted to be like him because he was a brilliant boxer. It was only later when I watched the documentaries and read the books that I learned about the other stuff. How he refused the draft into the United States army during the Vietnam War, how he converted to Islam. That made Ali a political figure, a different kind of role model for kids. Ali's situation was different from mine. He chose to be a political person. He grew up at a difficult time for blacks in America. The decisions he made were all to do with that. He refused to fight because his faith forbade him to kill innocent people. He no longer saw America's war as his war. It was deep stuff. But it was through sport that he made a difference and gained influence.

I would never say that I was as important a person as Ali in boxing or anything else. I'm not even trying to be like him, though if people want to say I fight like him that is OK by me. But I am inspired by what he did, by his bravery. And there are days, when I see how people from the Pakistani community look up to me, that I feel very proud. That is how he must have felt. I have become a representative in a way, a positive symbol of Asian culture for hundreds of thousands of people in Bolton and the rest of Britain, just as Ali was for black people in America.

And all because of sport. I've lost count of the number of times people I have never met approach me in Bolton. Once I was just sitting in the car, chilling, when a woman came up to me and kissed me. She told me that she prayed for me whenever I fight, that she loved me like a son. It was mad. I had never seen her in my life before. She was a Muslim woman looking up to me. That gave me strength. My religion gives me strength, and influences everything I do.

I believe my faith is as important in my success as my talent as a boxer. A lot of people say the two don't go together. If Islam says violence is wrong, how can you box? That's not how I see it. Boxing is a sport. It has rules. It teaches discipline and respect. In that way learning to box went hand in hand with learning the Koran. Learning the Arabic way of praying was tough. You had to sacrifice your time. It taught me discipline. It gave me a different outlook on life. All those things helped me with my boxing growing up – sacrifice, discipline, respect. To get on at the mosque and do well with your learning, and in the ring, you have to be dedicated. For example at Ramadan, you are not allowed to take food or water between sunrise and sunset. When you are training for fights that can be difficult. But I turn it to my advantage. I am making the sacrifice for Allah. That makes me stronger. I was training for the Gethin fight during Ramadan. I actually put more into it. It was very hard but by denying myself I was showing my commitment to my God and to my sport.

There are loads of important lessons I have taken with me from the Koran into my life as a professional boxer. At seventeen I felt I understood the teachings of the Koran much better. I had read it twice by then and had a more mature understanding of the holy book. That helped me all the way through the Olympics and now when I fight. I pray before every bout. I pray with my mum in the hotel before going to the venue and again in the ring before the fight. It's all private stuff. None of it is done for show.

I just ask Allah for strength in the fight, then when the bell goes I get on with it.

As this book was going to print the finishing touches were being made to our new mosque in Bolton. It is probably a mile from the Medina. It cost £700,000 to build. That's a lot of money for 300 members to find. Each mosque has its own membership. Every member of our mosque had to contribute £1,000 to the building costs. You could pay more if you wanted to. The rest came from fundraising in the town and outside Bolton. There were no handouts from the council, no grants, no Lottery money. That takes a massive commitment and shows how public-spirited the Muslim community is. I was asked to lay the first brick. It was a massive honour for me. Usually important people, scholars, teachers or businessmen are honoured in this way, but our mosque chose me. That shows how important I have become as a role model for my community. That's a big responsibility. I try my best every day to be a good person, to be a good Muslim, and to be as normal as possible. I don't drink. I don't do drugs. I can't ever see myself taking the wrong path like a lot of famous people do. My family, and my faith would never let that happen.

When I have finished boxing and have a family of my own my kids will do the same as I did, as my brother and sisters, our cousins. They will go to the new mosque and study the Koran. Hopefully it will do for them what it has done for me, show them how to be good people, proud of their heritage and respectful to others. And it will be cool for them to see my name written on that first brick.

Acknowledgements

My heartfelt thanks to my mum and dad, my sisters Tabinda and Mariyah and to my brother Haroon for his services as a punch bag; to my uncles Terry and Taz, who have been with me every step of the way, to my cousins, my gran Iqbal Begum who is no longer with us but always in my heart, and grandad Lall Khan who died before I was born. Without them, I wouldn't have a story to tell.

Thanks also to my first boxing coach, Tommy Battle, for getting me started; to Tony Smith and Mick Jelley at Bolton Lads & Girls Club and Bury ABC respectively for making my Olympic dream possible and to the staff and coaches of the Amateur Boxing Association: Paul King, Ian Irwin, Terry Edwards and Jim Davidson for taking an Olympian risk on a young boxer.

I will always be grateful to Mr Dickinson for the encouragement he gave me during my time at Smithills School in Bolton, and to Graham Roberts for his support at Bolton Community College.

A big thank you goes to my promoter Frank Warren, his partner Ed Simons and the rest of the staff at Sports Network for making my first year as a professional so special; to my trainer Oliver Harrison, corner man Jed and Bolton Wanderers' sports science team for their expertise, time and patience; to my business manager Asif Vali and legal eagle Robert Davis, who have all worked tirelessly for the cause.

Finally, a warm salute to my mates who followed me through the amateurs all the way to Athens: Maj, Ayaz, Mat, Khushi, Jav, RC, Nigel, Khalid, Wilber, George, Basit, Bash, Sonu, Perkins, Duba, Saj, Pecky, Earl, Nasar, Langley, Jerry and Dave McDonald.

Career Record

Amir Khan's Professional Boxing Record

Date	Opponent	Event	Result
2006			
8 July	Colin Bain	Millenium Stadium, Wales	WON RSC 2
20 May	Laszlo Komjathi	Belfast, Northern Ireland	WON PTS 6
25 February	Jackson Williams	London ExCel Centre, England	WON RSC 3
28 January	Vitali Martynov	Nottingham Arena, England	WON RSC 1
2005			
12 December	Daniel Thorpe	London ExCel Centre, England	WON RSC 2
5 November	Steve Gethin	Braehead Arena, Glasgow, Scotland	WON RSC 3
10 September	Baz Carey	Cardiff International Arena, Wales	WON PTS 4
16 July	David Bailey	Bolton Arena, England	WON RSC 1

Amir Khan's Amateur Boxing Record

Date	Opponent	Event	Result
2005			
14 May	Mario Kindelan (CUB)	Fight Night, Bolton (Cuba vs England)	WON 4 (19–13)
18 February	Steve Williams (ENG)	ABA Championship	RSC 3
7 February	Craig Watson (ENG)	ABA Championship	WON 4 (21–9)
7 February	Liam Dorian (ENG)	ABA Championship	WON 4 (23–4)
2004			
3 December	Michael Evans (USA)	USA vs England Dual	WON 4 (35–13)
29 August	Mario Kindelan (CUB)	Olympic Games Final	LOST 4 (22–30)
27 August	Serik Yeleuov (KAZ)	Olympic Games Semi-Final	WON 4 (40–26)
24 August	Jong-Sub Baik (KOR)	Olympic Games Quarter-Final	WON 4 RSC 1
20 August	Dimitar Shtilianov (BUL)	Olympic Games Second Round	WON 4 (37–21)
16 August	Marios Kaperonis (GRE)	Olympic Games First Round	WON RSC 3

AMIR KHAN'S AMATEUR BOXING RECORD

Date	Opponent	Event	Result
2004			
18 June	Zokir Artikov (UZB)	World Junior Championships Final	WON 4 (30–16) Gold medal
17 June	Alexis Vastine (FRA)	World Junior Championships Semi-Final	RSC 1
16 June	Darkhan Azirov (KAZ)	World Junior Championships Quarter-Final	WON 4 (36–20)
14 June	Jorge Hernandez (CUB)	World Junior Championships	WON 4 (21–6)
12 June	Sheng Liao (ROC)	World Junior Championships	RSC 1
26 May	Mario Kindelan (CUB)	Acropolis Cup (Pre Olympic Tournament)	LOST 4 (13–33)
4 April	Rovsham Huseinov (AZE)	Strandja Cup Final (2nd Olympic Qualifier)	WON Gold medal
3 April	Adrian Alexandru (RUM)	Strandja Cup Semi-Final (2nd Olympic Qualifier)	WON 4 (46–27)
2 April	Bagrat Avojan (ARM)	Strandja Cup Quarter-Final (2nd Olympic Qualifier)	RSC 3
1 April	Avdantil Kashia (GEO)	Strandja Cup (2nd Olympic Qualifier)	WON 4 40–18)
20 February	Avdantil Kashia (GEO)	European Senior Championship (1st Olympic Qualifier)	LOST 4 (20–29)

Date	Opponent	Event	Result
2004			
11 January	Arthur Schmidt (GER)	Senior Adidas Boxing Gala	WON 4 (56–39)
10 January	Martin Dressen (GER)	Senior Adidas Boxing Gala	RSC 3 Gold medal
9 January	Enrico Wagner (GER)	Senior Adidas Boxing Gala	WON 4 (30–20)
2003			
15 November	Sen Cihat (TUR)	European Youth Championships	WON Gold medal
12 November	Sergy Shutov (RUS)	European Youth Championships	RSC 1
11 November	Balazs Bacskai (HUN)	European Youth Championships	WON 3 (23–7)
9 August	Nurlam Mamedov (AZE)	European Cadet Championships	RSC 3 (20–5) Gold medal
7 August	Artem Subotin (RUS)	European Cadet Championships	WON 3 (34–26)
6 August	V. Catujanschi (MOL)	European Cadet Championships	RSC 1 (19–4)
4 August	S. Jomardoshvili (GEO)	European Cadet Championships	WON 3 (27–12)

AMIR KHAN'S AMATEUR BOXING RECORD

Date	Opponent	Event	Result
2003			
3 July	Victor Ortiz (USA)	International Junior Olympic Tournament	RSC 2 Gold medal
2 July	Anthony Medrano (USA)	International Junior Olympic Tournament	RSC 1
1 July	Emanuelle Ortíz (PUR)	International Junior Olympic Tournament	RSC 1
24 May	N. Smedley (ENG)	ABA National Junior	Gold Medal
19 May	V. Mantel (ALE)	Germany vs England Youth Dual	RSC
10 May	S. Welsh (ENG)	National Juniors Finals	WON
30 March	S. McDonnagh (ENG)	Northwest and Northeast Youth Championships	RSC
1 March	C. Wood (ENG)	Northwest and Northeast Youth Championships	RSC 3
15 February	M. Ungi (ENG)	Scholastic Championship Counties of the Northwest	WON Gold Medal
10 February	J. Keenan (ENG)	Regional Youth Championship	WON 3
18 January	L. Roberts (ENG)	Regional Youth Championship	RSC

Date	Opponent	Event	Result
2002			
13 December	M. Poston (ENG)	Club Fight	RSC
9 November	D. Appleby (ENG)	Club Fight	RSC
2 November	B. Saunders (ENG)	Club Fight	WON 3
10 October	J. Davidson (ENG)	Club Fight	WON 3
6 July	M. Forde (IRL)	Four Nations Cadet Tournament	RSC 1 Gold medal
5 July	G. McManus (SCO)	Four Nations Cadet Tournament	RSC 3
15 March	R. Perron (ENG)	Club Fight	WON
10 March	S. Turner (ENG))	ABA Youth Championship (Class 3)	KO 1 Gold medal
23 February	B. Cunningham (ENG)	National Youth Championships	RSC
7 February	D. Simms (ENG)	Northwestern Counties Youth Championship	RSC
21 January	T. Bowker (ENG))	Northwestern Counties Youth Championship	WON 3
January	J. Keenan (ENG)	Northwestern Counties Youth Championship	WON 3 unanimous

AMIR KHAN'S AMATEUR BOXING RECORD

Date	Opponent	Event	Result
2001			
15 December	Francis Foley (ENG)	Club Fight	WON 3 unanimous
30 November	P. Lockhart (IRL)	England vs Ireland Youth Dual	WON 3
10 November	M. Taliya (DAN)	Hancock Cup	WON 3 (5–0)
19 October	C. Fleming (ENG)	Unknown	RSC 2
13 May	J. Sweeney (IRL)	England vs Ireland Youth Dual	WON 3 unanimous
28 April	B. Page (ENG)	National Youth Championships	WON 3 Gold medal
19 February	A. Henderson (ENG)	National Youth Championships	RSC
10 February	D. Ward (ENG)	National Youth Championships	(Class B)
February	J. Kennedy (ENG)	Northwest Counties Youth Championships	RSC 2
28 January	W. Warburton (ENG)	Club Fight	RSC
12 January	S. Worthington (ENG)	Club Fight	RSC

AMIR KHAN

Date	Opponent	Event	Result
2000			
9 December	D. Clark (ENG)	Club Fight	RSC
24 November	D. McAdam (SCO)	England vs Scotland Youth Dual	WON 3
10 November	Adam King (ENG)	Club Fight	LOST 3
28 October	T. Downes (ENG)	Multi Nations Youth Championships	WON
27 October	G. Buckland (ENG)	Multi Nations Youth Championships	WON
22 May	Adam King (ENG)	Club Fight	LOST 3
28 April	J. Aray (ENG)	North vs Middle (region of England) Championships	WON 3
13 April	Adam King (ENG)	Club Fight	WON 3
18 March	R. Ward (ENG)	ABA Junior (Class A) Championships	LOST 3
3 March	N. N. Botton (ENG)	North (Zone) Youth Championships	WON 3
19 Feburary	L. Atkin (ENG)	Northwestern Counties Championship	WON
12 Feburary	C. Sheerin (ENG)	Northwestern Counties Championship	WON 3
4 January	S. Worthington (ENG)	Northwestern Counties Championship	WON

AMIR KHAN'S AMATEUR BOXING RECORD

Date	Opponent	Event	Result
1999			
6 December	D. Clark (ENG)	Club Fight	WON 3
29 November	C. Buller (ENG)	Club Fight	WON 3
10 October	M. Unsworth (ENG)	Club Fight	WON 3
3 October	R. Ward (ENG)	Club Fight	WON 3
27 May	S. Parnall (ENG)	Club Fight	WON 3
20 April	M. Pardoe (ENG)	Club Fight	WON 3
14 April	M. K. Donohoe (ENG)	Club Fight	WON 3
1 April	M. Unsworth (ENG)	Club Fight	WON 3
15 March	M. Unsworth (ENG)	Club Fight	WON 3
9 March	Richard Beach (ENG)	Club Fight	WON 3
4 March	T. Doran (ENG)	Club Fight	WON 3
5 February	J. Brattley (ENG)	Club Fight	WON 3
1 January	B. Whitehurst (ENG)	Club Fight	WON 3

AMIR KHAN

Date	Opponent	Event	Result
1998			
11 December	M. Unsworth (ENG)	Club Fight	LOST 3
1 November	D. Halsall (ENG)	Club Fight	WON 3
28 May	B. Yates (ENG)	Club Fight	LOST 3
4 May	M. Palmer (ENG)	Club Fight	LOST 3
5 April	M. Unsworth (ENG)	Club Fight	LOST 3
3 March	J. Morley (ENG)	Club Fight	RSC
7 February	G. Hyde (ENG)	Club Fight	WON 3
1997			
12 December	M. J. JONES (ENG)	Club Fight	WON 3

KO: Knockout
RSC: Referee stopped contest
PTS: Points

Index

ABA 26, 42, 96, 107
  Championships 5, 30, 76, 88, 90–93
  Junior Championship 24, 25
  Khan's amateur package 88
  Khan's row with 28, 91–5
  Olympic selection 30–32, 34, 35, 37
Adidas 40
Adidas Boxing Gala 33–4
AIBA 16
Ali, Muhammad ix, 13, 22, 106, 112, 129, 185
Allardyce, Sam 99, 116, 122, 164
Anderson, Jimmy 143
Anfield 125
Arum, Bob 89
Ash (college friend) 65, 72, 76
Asif, *see* Vali, Asif
Astley Bridge cricket club 143, 144
Athens 88–9, 122
  see also Olympic Games 2004
Aziz, Shaista 146–53

Bahamas 128
Bailey, David 112, 113, 114, 116–17

Bain, Colin 4
Barnes, John 125
Battagram, Pakistan 152
Battle, Tommy 12, 13, 14
BBC 52, 53, 87, 96
Becker, Boris 124
Beckham, David 53, 123–4, 125, 171
Belfast 118–19, 131
Benn, Nigel 99
Bernath, Clive 5
Beshenivsky, Sharon 130
Bingham, Ensley 23, 110
Blackpool 165
Blair, Tony 59
Bolton 3, 24, 64, 81, 158, 163–4, 167
  Asian community 69, 83–5, 172, 178, 181, 184–5, 187
  Khan family arrives 8, 134–7
  Khan fights 95, 97–100, 107, 114–17
  Khan's gym 176
  Khan's reception 58–9, 63
  mayor of 147
Bolton Association 136
Bolton Community College 4, 61, 63–76, 130, 140–41

Bolton Evening News 24, 62
Bolton Indian cricket club 142
Bolton Lads Club 13, 14, 89, 125
Bolton Town Hall 63
Bolton Wanderers FC 122–3, 130
Botham, Ian 136
Bowker, T. 25–6
Boxing News 5
Bradford 3, 78, 82, 130–31
Branson, Sir Richard 128–9
British Aerospace 82, 135
Brownlow Fold Junior School 10, 170
Buckingham Palace 59
Bulgaria 36, 67
Burke, Stephen 35
Bury 64
Bury ABC 18–19, 21, 28, 61, 89, 94, 140, 157, 171

Calzaghe, Joe 96
Cardiff 4
Carey, Baz 118
Carolyn (physio) 45
Champions League 165
Champs Camp, Manchester 110, 112
Chowdery, Nabeel 145, 146, 148
Clark, D. 22
Commonwealth Games 39, 88, 95
Coronation Street 18, 125, 127, 130, 172
cricket 21, 62, 79, 126, 136, 142–4
Croatia 35, 49, 55
Cuba 94–5, 98, 128–30
Cyprus 47, 53

Daily Mirror 150–51, 154, 173
Dalglish, Kenny 125
David, Craig 124
Davidson, Jim 40

De La Hoya, Oscar ix, 89
Dickinson, Mr (PE teacher) 27, 61–3
Dolan, Mick 87, 90
Dorian, Liam 91
Dubai 141, 166

Edmonds, Chris 44
Edwards, Terry 31–4, 36–7, 41, 42, 47–53, 56–7, 97, 106–7
Edwards, Terry Jnr 57
Egan, Joe 164
Elite Sports Management 89
Elizabeth II, Queen 59, 76
Emms, Gail 47
England (boxing) 23, 90, 94, 95, 103–4
   junior squad 25, 26, 28, 29, 31
England (cricket) 144
England (football) 1, 4, 6
England Academy 143
European Cadets Championships 31
European Junior Championships 39
European Schoolboys Championships 32
Evans, Jim 90
Evans, Michael 90

Farnworth 139
Ferdinand, Rio 123
Ferguson, Sir Alex 123
Flintoff, Andrew (Freddie) 21, 99, 109, 126
football 122–3, 125, 128, 130–31, 165
Foreman, George 185
Fosse, Ernie 111
Foster, Steve 110
France 47
Frazier, Joe ix, 106, 185

Gaskell Street Primary School,
    Bolton 135
Gavin, Frankie 39, 94, 98
Germany 33–5
Gerrard, Steven 4
Gethin, Steve 145, 146, 186
Giannakopoulos, Stelios 122
Giggs, Ryan 123
Glasgow 167, 173
GMR 64
Gohar (brother-in-law) 84, 159–60
Golden Boy Promotions 89
Graham, Billy 104, 110, 112
Granada Reports 158
Grange-over-Sands 142
Grant, Michael 5–6, 98
Great Yarmouth 91–2, 93
Greater Manchester Finals 25

Hakkinen, Mika 124
Halliwell Boxing Club, Bolton
    11–13, 24, 108, 169
Halsall, Dean 21
Hamed, Naseem 23–4, 54, 96,
    112
Harrison, Audley ix, 49, 51–2,
    53, 96
Harrison, Oliver x, 1, 104–6,
    109–13, 115, 118–19, 168
Hart, Colin 106
Hart, Gary 16
Hart, John 14, 16
Hatton, Ricky 23, 96–7, 104,
    112, 174
Hayes, Peter 44
Hearn, Barry 90, 96
Hernandez, Jorge 44
Hobson, Dennis 90, 96
Hollyoaks 125, 172
Holmes, Kelly 46, 57, 124
Hughes, Brian 104
Hussain, Hasib 177

India 143
Ingram, Vincent 138–9
Ipswich 24
Irani, Ronnie 60, 62, 140
Ireland 94
Irwin, Ian 31, 32, 42, 43, 53, 54
Islam 3, 179–86
    Koran 182–4, 186
Islamabad, Pakistan 78, 147, 153
Istanbul 165–6
Italy 32, 40
ITN 150
ITV 95, 96, 107, 116, 165

Jed (trainer) 115, 119
Jelley, Mick 35, 91, 115, 132, 142
    attitude to boxing 40, 99, 112
    and Khan's career 29, 37, 86,
        90, 97
    Khan's coach 18–22, 26, 27,
        60, 103–4, 106, 157
Jelley, Peter 19
Jewell, Paul 130, 131
Jones, Danny 125–6
Jones, Mark 14–15
Jowell, Tessa 59
Junior Olympics (Louisiana,
    2003) 29, 30, 65

Kashmir 147
Kay, Peter 164
Kay, Vernon 164
Keane, Roy 123
Keegan, Kevin 125
Kendall 16
Khan, Amir:
    ambitions 22, 65–6, 84, 87
    appearance 164; hair 170–72;
        physique 13, 14, 20, 25, 38
    as athlete 27, 61, 63
    birth and childhood 7–11, 139,
        170, 181–2

as boxer 34–5, 76, 86–90, 95–
6; amateur fights 14–18, 21–
3, 25–6, 30, 51, 97–100,
192–9, *see also* Olympic
Games; commercial deals 40,
121, 153–5; defeats 17–18,
21–2, 28, 36; fitness 67–8,
113; footwork 13;
internationals 24, 26, 29;
joins gym 11–12; love of
boxing 14, 20–22, 65, 84,
167; management office 121,
140; professional career 4,
29, 107, 111–12, 114–18,
191; reputation 27; sparring
sessions 12–13, 32–3, 113;
stamina 27; training 33, 62,
108–12, 167; turns
professional 96–7, 100–101,
107, 167–8
cars 63, 101–2, 124, 168, 172;
accidents 8–9, 154, 173–4;
driving lessons and test 102,
157–62
celebrity status 67, 109–10,
114, 120–33, 164–6; in
Athens 52–4; in Bolton 40–
41, 57–9, 74–5, 158; fan
mail 24
charity fund-raising 125, 130–
33, 145–7, 150, 152
education: college 64–76;
school 10, 20–21, 23, 27,
60–4, 84
family background 3, 8, 77–9,
81–3
injuries 8–9, 44–6, 52, 87
involvement with police
173–5
and money 35, 88, 101, 168
as Muslim x–xi, 2–3, 108,
177–87

personality 20, 74; confidence
22, 28, 34, 43, 49, 53, 114,
117; discipline 71, 186;
fighting spirit 7, 10–11, 27,
36, 41, 49; headstrong 43;
humility xi; tearaway 7–8, 10
social life 83–4, 162, 172–3;
girls 1, 83–5; mates 164–6,
167, 168–9
website 112, 176
Khan, Anwar 136
Khan, Haroon (brother) 1, 3, 8,
28, 63, 115, 144, 147, 171,
174–5
Khan, Iqbal Begum (grandmother)
7–11, 82, 137, 139, 141
Khan, Lall (grandfather) 3, 8, 77–
8, 81–3, 134–5, 137, 139,
140
Khan, Mariyah (sister) 8
Khan, Mrs (mother) 11, 62–3,
83, 84, 124, 127, 157, 186
Khan, Shah (father) 58, 75, 83,
119, 132, 137–40
background 8, 32
introduces Amir to boxing 3,
11, 15, 18
manages Amir's career 31, 34–
5, 37, 43, 86, 88–90, 92–7,
111–12, 121, 155
marriage 84, 139
and Pakistan 78–80, 81
travels with Amir 4, 14, 26, 30,
38, 47, 108, 115–16, 140,
147
work 8, 35, 79, 90, 138–40
Khan, Tabinda (sister) 8, 9, 84,
121, 139, 140, 160
Khan, Tahir (Taz, uncle) 7–9,
139, 140–42, 152, 166, 170,
172
Amir's relationship with 141

involvement in Amir's early
career 14, 16–18, 24, 37, 47,
97, 143
runs Amir's diary 121, 130,
131–2, 140, 142
work 141–21
Kilpatrick, Greg 157–61
Kindelan, Mario x, 5, 15, 44,
128, 129
Athens Olympics 41–2, 48, 55–
6, 75
Bolton bout 24, 94–100, 104,
106, 107
King, Adam 22
King, Don 89
King, Paul 91–2, 93, 94, 95
King's Hall, Belfast 118, 131
Komjathi, Laszlo 118, 130, 171
Korea 42, 43, 46, 52, 87

Lancashire Cricket Club 21, 126–
7, 143, 144
Langley, Darren 47
Laureus Awards 123
Leonard, Sugar Ray ix, 129
Lewis, Lennox ix, 54, 112
Lillee, Dennis 144
Little, Ralph 123
Liverpool 16, 17, 22–3, 90, 91
Liverpool FC 125, 165
London bombings (July 2005) 2–
3, 25, 145, 177, 180
Louis, Joe 19
Louisiana 30, 65

Macdonald, Dave 21
Magilton, David 24
Mahmood, Mrs (aunt) 173
Mahmood, Rakeb (cousin) 9, 21,
65, 144, 159, 160
Mahmood, Sahid (Terry, uncle)
134–9, 170, 179

at Amir's fights 14, 16
cricket interests 142–3
work 8, 82
Mahmood, Sajid (cousin) 16, 173
childhood 9, 21, 136–7, 170
as cricketer 21, 126–7, 142–4
at school 60, 61–2
Maj (friend) 16, 166
Manchester 17, 23, 25–6, 35, 57–
8, 96, 104, 110
Manchester United FC 122–3,
127–8
Martin, Phil 110, 112
Matore, Pakistan 3, 32, 77–81,
83, 84, 138, 147
McGuigan, Barry 118, 124
McGuinness, Paddy 164
media 1, 3, 58, 93, 150, 155;
local 24, 40, 63; national
press 91, 51; negative stories
153–5; press conferences 49,
75, 113–14, 118–19, 153;
TV 58, 74, 158
Medina Mosque, Bolton 181–3,
187
Messias, Matt 123
Miandad, Javed 136
Middelton, Manchester 18
Midland Hotel, Manchester 97,
110, 124
Midlands Doctors Association
133
Mo (sparring partner) 113
Moods restaurant, Bolton 173
Moore, Jamie 104–5, 109
Morley, Jack 16–17
Morrison's, Bolton 157
Moschino 121
Mullready, Vinny 139
Murray, Andy 166–7
Muzaffarabad, Pakistan 133, 147,
148, 151, 152

National Youth Championships (2000) 22–3
Nazar, Mudassar 136
Nicholls, Paul 60
Nolan, Kevin 122
North College, Bolton 65
Northern Ireland xi, 180
Northside Club, Manchester 25–6
Northwestern Counties 25–6
Nottingham 132

Okocha, Jay-Jay 122
Old Trafford 17, 23, 126
Oliver's Gym, Salford 108–9, 167, 169, 176
Olympic Games x, 31, 66
  2000 Sydney 49
  2004 Athens xi, 2, 5–6, 15, 29, 46–56, 75, 86–8, 90, 113; ABA selections 30–35; homecoming of British team 57; Khan's bouts 48–56, 99, 100; Pre-Olympic Tournament 41–2; qualifiers 35–40, 55, 67, 69, 88, 113; training camp 47, 67
  2008 Beijing 31, 56, 65, 87, 89, 90
  2012 London 28, 59, 123
  see also Junior Olympics
Ortiz, Victor 30
Oxfam 146, 147, 149, 150–54

Pakistan 3, 8, 32, 77–81, 135, 137, 139, 159
  earthquake (2005) 130, 133, 145–56
Palmer, M. 17–18
Perkins, Neil 47, 50
Phillips, Billy 95
Pinsent, Matthew 47, 57
Plovdiv, Bulgaria 36

Pope, Philip 49
Portsmouth 106
Portugal 123
Powell, Dean 111–12
Press Association 93
Preston 25, 74
Preston Guildhall 91

Queen's Park, Bolton 169, 174

racism 8, 26, 178
Radcliffe, Paula 46, 47, 63–4
Ranby prison, Nottingham 132–3
Rawalpindi, Pakistan 81, 83
Rawtenstall 16, 141
Reebok 121, 153–5
Reebok Stadium, Bolton 90, 95, 100, 107, 115, 122–3
Reid, Robin 104
Repton ABC 22–3
Roberts, Graham 4, 63–4, 66–72, 75–6
Robertson, Nathan 47
Ronaldo, Cristiano 123
Rooney, Wayne 1, 3, 25, 87
Ruddock, Razor 125
Rumble in the Jungle 13, 185
Rush, Ian 125
Russia 23

Saj (friend) 115, 124–5, 131, 132, 164–6
  appearance 164, 172
  cars and driving 46, 157, 159
  college mate 65, 66, 68, 72, 73, 75–6
  home 172
  Indian background 170, 172
Salford 107–8
Savon, Felix 128, 129
Scholes, Paul 123
School Shuttle Childcare Services 46

Scotland (juniors) 25
Seconds Out website 5
SFX 121
Sharapova, Maria 53
Sheffield 32, 35
Simons, Ed 95, 96
Siz (Shiraz, barber) 170–72
Skelton, Matt 100
Sky TV 63–4, 96, 126
Smith, Alan 123
Smithills School, Bolton 60–63,
    65, 72, 73, 140
Spain 122, 123
Spikey, Dave 60
Sports Personality of the Year
    Awards 166
Stallone, Sylvester 75
Stevenson, Teofilo 128, 129
Stoke-on-Trent 14, 15, 143
Sun 106, 158, 165, 173
Sunday Times 151, 153–5
Superstars 122, 123

terrorism 2–3, 177–80, 183
Thai boxing 110, 114
Thompson, Carl 110
Thorpe, Daniel 147
Thrilla in Manilla 183
Tiber, Vitali 34
Trafford Centre, Manchester 164
Tszyu, Kostya 97
Tyson, Mike 109, 110, 120, 124–
    5

United States 89, 90
Universum 34–5, 88
Unsworth, Mark 17, 21

Vali, Asif 46, 89, 91–2, 94–7, 115,
    119, 121, 125, 128, 140
Vaughan, Michael 126
Virgin Active, Bolton 108
Virgin Airways 128

Walters, Keith 42–3
Ward, Bobby 22–3
Warren, Frank 89–90, 94–7, 100,
    104–5, 107, 111
Watkinson, Mike 126
Watson, Craig 91
West Bolton 142
Whitecroft School, Bolton 136
Wigan Athletic FC 130
Williams, Danny 100
Williams, Gareth 89
Williams, Steve 91
Williams, Venus 53
World Cadet Championships
    (2003) 29, 30, 42
World Championships (Belfast,
    2001) 56
World Junior Championships 42–
    6, 87
World Cup (soccer, 2006) 1, 3–4,
    6, 172, 184

Yates, Ben 18